Social Change in
Russia and Eastern Europe

Social Change in
Russia and Eastern Europe

*From Party Hacks
to Nouveaux Riches*

Silviu Brucan

Westport, Connecticut
London

Library of Congress Cataloging-in-Publication Data

Brucan, Silviu, 1916–
    Social change in Russia and Eastern Europe : from party hacks to
nouveaux riches / Silviu Brucan.
       p.   cm.
    Includes bibliographical references and index.
    ISBN 0–275–96322–5 (alk. paper)
      1. Post-communism—Russia (Federation) 2. Post-communism—
Europe, Eastern.   3. Russia (Federation)—Social conditions.
4. Europe, Eastern—Social conditions.   I. Title.
HN530.2.A8B78   1998
306´.0947—dc21   98–14925

British Library Cataloguing in Publication Data is available.

Library of Congress Catalog Card Number: 98–14925
ISBN: 0–275–96322–5

First published in 1998

Praeger Publishers, 88 Post Road West, Westport, CT 06881
An imprint of Greenwood Publishing Group, Inc.

Printed in the United States of America

∞™

The paper used in this book complies with the
Permanent Paper Standard issued by the National
Information Standards Organization (Z39.48–1984).

10 9 8 7 6 5 4 3 2 1

Contents

Introduction

This book is like an adventuresome expedition in a tropical forest. To this day nobody has ventured to write a *social* history of the transition from "state socialism" (more state than socialism) to the post-communist society. The reason is simple: we are dealing here with a social transformation without precedent, a historical U-turn of 180 degrees from socialism to capitalism dictated by the integration into the world system characteristic of the late twentieth century. Therefore, no theory is available that could direct its course and provide a deeper explanation of the necessary social changes and of their succession. *Terra incognita* by all means.

And yet, the *social*, as the most stable, enduring, and coherent facet of the historical process, could tell us better than the *political* or *economic* one about the state of a society and where it is heading. Unlike political and economic developments, social structures are seldom affected by accidents or crises such as the death of a strong leader or a stock market crash. Social structures are more resilient; they change very slowly, and thus are more predictable. Hence, when the question arises whether the process of change in Poland and

Romania, or for that matter in Russia, is reversible, political scientists and economists are forced to qualify their answer with all kinds of "ifs" that they cannot predict. It is the slow but powerful flow of the social river that can more reliably tell us the answer.

To discover the nature of the social landscape of Eastern European nations today, if and how the new social structure has taken shape, we must first find out what the social reality was under the communist regime, so cosmetically presented by official history and so superficially investigated by sociologists. After all, people are the same; they did not vanish in the revolution, and what we have to do is to see whether and how they have changed under the impact of the economic reform and policy decisions. What, in reality, was that working class described as the ruling force in society? What about the collective peasants? Did they lose the instinct of land ownership, as Marxism-Leninism wanted us to believe? And, of course, the most fascinating study concerns the power elite, the so-called *nomenklatura*, whose most versatile members have passed with staggering dexterity from the offices of the party's Central Committee right into the governing boards of big corporations or private banks, turning into the most zealous advocates of wild capitalism.

A clear distinction should be made between social developments in Russia and those in Central Europe, a distinction originating far back in the pre-communist societies and marvelously preserved in the latter, even under the uniformitarian pressure of Stalinism. The name of that distinction is *middle class*. In Central Europe 20% to 30% of the active population used to enjoy a middle-class type of material subsistence and life style (house ownership, automobile, cultural activities, travel abroad, and the like), which now have proven essential in building a market economy. In retrospect, we realize now that the "Prague Spring," as well as the strong reform movements in Hungary and Poland, reflected middle-class aims for liberalization and market rather than typical working-class grievances. Conversely, Russia seems to have been always one social class behind the historical process. In October 1917, when a socialist revolution was the problem, the social agent of change was missing—the *proletariat*. Today, when the problem is setting up a market economy, it is the *middle class* that is missing. There were, of course, in 1917 a few capitalists in Moscow and St. Petersburg, but after seventy years of communism not a trace of Russian bourgeois remained. Russia had to start from scratch, and this is why economic reform has been so daunting a task over there.

The data presented in chapter 3 show that there is an almost mathematical relationship between the percentage of a potential middle class before 1989 and the performance of the market reform today. *The middle class is the key factor in the market reform of post-communist societies.*

Romania is a special case in Eastern Europe. Unlike Poland, Hungary, and Czechoslovakia, where the presence of two political factors (a reformist wing in the communist party and an organized opposition outside the party) allowed for negotiations that resulted in a peaceful revolution and a *center-right* government, in Romania the Ceausescu dictatorship did not permit either of the two factors to take shape. As a result, the revolution was violent and a *center-left* government took power. Precisely because the Iliescu regime was not reformist and failed to initiate bold market-oriented measures, 1990 and 1991 were years in which the old social structure simplistically defined by Stalin (two classes, workers and peasants, plus one social category, the intelligentsia) remained petrified.

Nothing happened sufficiently strong to shake it. In the middle of 1991, under the pressure of the Council of Europe rather than that of internal forces, the Roman government initiated a reformist program: prices and foreign trade were liberalized, small enterprises and services were privatized, and an agrarian reform giving land to the peasants was enacted. This amounted to a kind of shock-therapy, and the old social forces reacted angrily: thousands of miners invaded Bucharest and toppled the Roman government. But the social effects of the market could not be halted, and, in 1992, Romania stepped into the *destructive stage of the old social structure*. The industrial workers declined numerically, their position and social prestige plummeted (not one single worker was appointed minister); the peasantry broke up according to the nature and magnitude of land ownership; new social forces emerged: a *middle class* in embryonic form and its superior stratum, an *upper class of* capitalists.

In the 1996 elections, the new social forces took an active part for the first time. One is reminded here that in Hungary, where market mechanisms had already been introduced in the 1960s, the two front-runners in the 1991 elections were both middle-class political parties. Conversely, in Russia the lack of an adequate-size middle class may help to explain why the reformist parties could not find a social base.

Currently, in Romania, the middle-class-in-the-making and the big capitalists are pushing the rightist parties to become more assertive in their program and political discourse, causing a significant shift even in the center-left governing coalition that was moving Romanian politics to the right. The fact is that the new tycoons now control newspapers, radio, and TV stations, and thus are becoming an important factor in molding public opinion and influencing the electorate.

In Romania also, the 1996 elections brought to power a coalition government with a strong *center-right* inclination. Since the coalition represents a compromise between Christian democrats and Social democrats, it is the pressure of external forces, Euro-Atlantic to be sure, that is pushing the new power to the center-right, and, thus, to market reform. But the key to reform is and remains the middle class.

Middle class is a new notion in Eastern Europe. Marxist-Leninists listed it high among the taboos, blaming it for the disproof of Marx's nineteenth-century prediction that future society will be made of two antagonistic classes: workers and capitalists. Hence, I devote a whole chapter to this class, its origins and socio-cultural features as they apply in our societies today. Experience in the type of Western society to which we are heading shows that the middle class, precisely because of its in-between position in society, is unable to rule either the government or the economy, albeit it provides leaders for both; nevertheless, the middle class is setting the tone in culture, arts, and the consumption patterns (creating the consumer society), while serving as the main audience for the mass media.

How was the middle class born in Romania? With forceps! The market economy could not possibly function with workers and peasants alone. Merchants and entrepreneurs, businessmen and intermediaries, salesmen and managers are a *must*. Therefore, the formation of a class made up of such people is both vital and urgent. We cannot afford to replicate the slow and gradual process of its genesis that took so many decades in the West. So, we are witnessing here a social birth abrupt, painful, forced, accelerated—contenders cutting their way through the loopholes of our rudimentary and inadequate legislation. A *wild middle class*, I call it.

In the less-developed and poor Romania a monthly income of $300 (the average weekly wage is $100) should be considered the threshold of the middle class. The following qualify as middle class: (1) high state dignitaries, senators and deputies, generals; (2) directors and board members of state economic enterprises and banks; (3) in the private sector: managers and directors of foreign companies, who are paid in dollars; owners of stores, restaurants, and workshops; shareholders; lawyers and other liberal professionals; (4) economic agents in the "underground economy" (38% of the gross national product according to the Romanian Intelligence Service). The total number is in the order of *hundreds of thousands* and is rapidly growing, which means the middle class is about to take center stage in Romanian society, already being the locomotive that is pushing consumption in durable goods, cars, apartments, land, and new housing construction. The middle class supports the tourist industry and patronizes fancy restaurants, casinos, and bars, where a menu costs the monthly minimum wage in industry.

But the most striking social outcome of the revolution in the East is the *making of a host of millionaires in just five years.* The novelty of that phenomenon stems from the peculiar condition of their genesis: *because in a communist society the accumulation of private capital was censured and illegal, the post-1989 capitalists made their fortune at the expense of state property and capital,* grabbing assets, machinery, real estate, and even social capital of state enterprises or commercial organizations. Where did these millionaires come from? How did they make it? I examined thoroughly their know-how and determined six ways and means that have been utilized. These are described in detail in chapter 3. To mention but one here: Directors of state factories set up a private annex firm run by a wife or son, gradually transferring to this annex-firm machinery, raw materials, and even contracts with third parties and bank credits guaranteed by state assets. Ultimately, the state enterprise goes bankrupt, while the private firm takes over its business and becomes prosperous. In 1990 and 1991, when most operations of that kind were executed on a large scale, there was no legal instrument to prevent it. Although we don't yet have statistics based on personal income, one can safely estimate the number of Romanian millionaires in the order of tens of thousands. Quite a few in so short a time!

In Russia, the middle class originated in the economic state apparatus. Interestingly, even those who have become businessmen and owners of private enterprises stubbornly keep their positions in the state bureaucracy and remain on the state's payroll. As for the upper-middle class, Russia, with its enormous riches and natural resources, qualifies in the vanguard of this historical plunder of state property, ushering into the world the biggest tycoons of the East. Of course, in the forefront of that large-scale robbery were the former party and state bureaucrats holding strategic positions that allowed them to operate fast and with great efficiency. The process in Russia started earlier with Gorbachev's perestroika of 1985.

Finally, a recent poll concerning the future of Romania reveals that 60% of citizens do not know where Romania is heading, while the remaining 40% are divided as follows: 16%—toward capitalism, 11%—toward Western socialism, 13%—to restoration of communism. In the last chapter, I argue that the making of the new social structure provides the best answer to that question and examine the issue in the context of recent developments in Eastern Europe and Russia.

One thing is certain: Russia's way will be different from that of Eastern and Central European nations.

1

Social Structure in Communist States

In communist countries the study of the power structure was taboo. Communist leaders employed such idyllic formulae as "people power" or "working-class power" and did not permit professors of "scientific socialism" and researchers to find out *who* was exercising power on behalf of the people or working class, who was making decisions in socialist states. In fact, they did not want known *how many* were making major decisions, simply because major decisions were made by *one person*—the Secretary General. Obviously, such a conclusion could hardly fit the notion of the "most advanced democracy."

However, in the years of Nikita Khruschev's "thaw," Soviet sociologists were allowed to tackle the issue of social structure; and, if we follow that path, we can also find out something about power structure in socialism. The All-Union Congress, which took place in Minsk in January 1966, provided the first major forum in which Stalin's simplistic scheme of Soviet society (two non-antagonistic classes—workers and peasants, plus one stratum—the intelligentsia) was reappraised. V. S. Semenov, a leading and rather orthodox specialist on social structure, stated that "the present scheme could no longer satisfy Soviet scholars." In fact, he gave expression to the dissatisfaction of sociologists for not being useful so long as they operated with a scheme in stark contrast with social reality. Tatiana Zaslavskaya, who had already broken the conformist front earlier, challenged the homogeneous egalitarian social model presented in official documents: "The social positions occupied by different strata and classes in socialist society can be represented in the form of a certain hierarchy in which some positions are regarded as higher than others." In other words, a social structure in which vertically differentiated social groups were arranged on a "ladder of social positions" was defined, cautiously but clearly.[1] Another sociologist, O. I. Shkaratan, focused on social inequality and discovered the existence within Soviet society of "groups of people unequal in social and economic terms." He argued that social inequalities must be studied "for the purpose of struggling for their elimination" and made the point that the inequality of social groups should not be seen only as a heritage of capitalism but also as being reproduced by socialism.[2]

Apparently, the new unorthodox approaches of the 1960s reflected the actual tensions, grievances, and conflicts generated by the deep social divisions existing in Soviet society that were surfacing with the weakening of Stalinist repression.

Summarizing the debates and studies published in Soviet journals after the Minsk conference, Zev Katz elaborated a scheme of Soviet stratification that identifies six major groups:

1. The *natchalniks* (rulers, leaders)—essentially the ruling social group
2. The *intelligentsia*—the highly educated specialists in various fields
3. The *white-collar employees*—service and technical non-manual workers of lesser education
4. The *manual workers*—ranging from unskilled to the highly skilled

5. The *kolkhoz peasants*—including both rank-and-file labor and the administrative staff and cooperative sector

6. The *privately employed*—hired and self-employed persons not drawing wages in the state and cooperative sectors.

Four of these groups are seen as "classes" and two—the white-collar employees and the privately employed—as strata, given that they lacked a sufficiently characteristic loading of class determinants.[3]

In Katz's view, the natchalniks are clearly a separate class, although in education, nominal salaries, prestige, and some other characteristics they are, on the average, not far from the intelligentsia. It is in function, not production or the provision of an essential service for the population but *social control of men*, that the natchalniks, the political rulers, are distinctive. Walter Connor emphasizes that "the natchalniks constitute not one among many strategic elites but the ruling class, the monopolizer of effective power." As a group, he goes on, they are aware of common interests, ready and able to defend them with coercive and normative resources and to control entry of candidates to their ranks. These are *aparatchikii* and state officials, from Brezhnev down to urban and provincial bosses, whose power, in Boris Meissner's apt phrase, "rests in the position they hold, while that of intelligentsia is rooted in the authority and prestige inherent in the functions it performs."[4]

I agree with Katz's and Connor's explicit differentiation of political functionaries holding power from the intelligentsia. Indeed, the latter were not, as a class, in the business of ruling society. What is more, in the Brezhnev era, intellectuals were viewed with suspicion not only in the USSR, but also throughout most of Eastern Europe. However, I disagree with them on two points: (1) the natchalniks were the ruling social group and not a ruling class; and (2) within that group I make a distinction between leadership and party apparat.

NOMENKLATURA: CLASS OR SOCIAL GROUP?

Quite a few authors consider the party bureaucracy (the Soviets used the term *apparat*) a class in its own right. The most famous among them, Milovan Djilas, maintains that the "New Class" is an ownership class. The new class is "made up of those who have special privileges and the economic preference because of the administrative monopoly they hold" and "the government both administers and distributes national property." The new class, or its executive organ—the party oligarchy—"both acts as the owner and is the owner,"[5] writes Djilas.

While I agree with the first part of the definition, that the party bureaucracy acts as the owner of the means of production, I cannot find in Djilas's book any evidence that it "is the owner." Indeed, the basic fault with his definition is the lack of economic determinants of a class. As the metamorphosis of that transition is central in this book, let us examine this aspect in detail:

1. Although the declared aim of the new class was not to acquire major material advantages and it was neither ideologically "kosher" nor legally possible for its members to grab "means of production," in Romania some leaders built or bought houses and accumulated wealth in cash, depositing it in foreign banks under names of relatives.

2. The bureaucrats did not have an economic basis of their own, founded on personal property, and therefore did not have a social status based on wealth, no lasting and stable place in the production process or in the economic system. They did not have the legal possibility to pass on to their descendants their income, their privileges, or their economic status, as capitalists could do in the West.

3. Historical evidence shows that bureaucrats in party or state leadership could be fired, demoted, or removed from office, with the loss of all advantages they enjoyed while in power, sometimes with the loss of their freedom and even of their lives.

To sum up, the party apparat did not and could not constitute a class in the sense this notion has in history. Nevertheless, as a rule, all those who used to hold commanding positions in the state system (government, administration, military commanders, and the state's coercive forces) were recruited from the apparat.

The apparat was, thus, an observable and differentiated interacting social group (some call it nomenklatura) in Soviet society. Made up of full-time party and government officials who ran all state institutions, civil and military, it could well be described as the *ruling social group* in the USSR. Its members, the cadres, moved back and forth between managerial-technical jobs and party positions, participating regularly in party meetings and courses for ideological indoctrination. The cohesive force of the group stemmed from the special social relations and status of its members, their position in the structure of power, their high salaries, and, particularly, from their access to a wide range of restricted benefits and privileges, all combining to set this social elite apart from the rest of the population. In 1980, total membership of the group in the USSR (central and local power) was estimated to be about 250,000; in Romania, around 20,000. This group ran an administrative machinery that represented 15% of the work force.

VACILLATIONS IN INTELLECTUAL POLICY

With regard to *intellectuals*, the history of communist regimes was marked by dramatic fluctuations in policy. At the beginning, Lenin had emphasized with great pride that the Soviet government had the largest intellectual membership in Europe. In cultural and artistic life, the 1920s was a decade of memorable variety and achievement. In the party's own intellectual life, in its press, academic institutions, and scholarly publications, with their vivid debates in economics, social theory, philosophy, and science, this period was what an American historian termed the "golden age of Marxist thought in the USSR."[6]

Despite the large cultural emigration to the West as a result of the revolution, the 1920s brought a remarkable explosion of artistic ferment and creativity in almost every field in the Soviet Union. Serghey Eisenstein, Constantine Stanislavski, and Vselovod Meyerhold revolutionized the theater and film, founding new schools in these arts. A great diversity of artists expressed their theories and visions in a dazzling array of forms. Above all, it was a time of experimentation, when modernism and the cultural avant-garde flourished spectacularly, if briefly, under the lenient reign of the Bolshevik Party. To mention but a few, Ernst Kandinski and Marc Chagall started painting in Russia before they fled to the West. In prose fiction and poetry, major works were written by Mikhail Sholohov, Isaak Babel, Valentin Kataev, Konstantin Fedin, Serghey Essenin, Vladimir Mayakovski, Anna Akhmatova, Boris Pasternak, Boris Pilniak, Mikhail Bulgakov, Osip Mandelstam, and Mikhail Zoshchenko. A complete list would be much longer, a virtual roster of the great names of Soviet literature, many of whom were to perish under Stalin's repression.

Initially, technical and scientific intellectuals also were attracted to the restoration of the country. However, this ended in the late 1920s when Stalin unleashed his terror against "bourgeois specialists" and staged his famous political trials that ended with death sentences.

After Stalin's death, a second cultural upsurge started under Khrushchev's celebrated "Thaw." Artists and writers vilified during the Stalin era were rehabilitated; and Soviet science was liberated from dogmatism, bringing great vitality in scientific research and theory. But very soon, in the Brezhnev era, the conservative policies in economic life were necessarily accompanied by a conservative backlash in cultural and artistic affairs, reinforced by recurrent efforts to rehabilitate Stalin.

As Eastern-European communist parties followed *grosso modo* the Communist Party of the Soviet Union's line, we found similar vacillations in intellectual policy all over the Eastern bloc. A certain peculiarity in this respect was apparent in Poland. In the 1970s, sociologist Jan Szczepanski conceived a four-class model of society based primarily on the traditional triad of class features: power, property (in the sense of income), and prestige. The model is shown below:

Intelligentsia

- creative intelligentsia
- highly educated professionals (academics, doctors, and so on)
- political officials
- civil servants
- economic managers
- ordinary white-collar functionaries

Manual workers (incorporating differences by skill levels, sector or branch location, and so on)

Peasantry

- independent peasant owners deriving a living from farming
- peasant-workers with mixed incomes
- peasant–white-collar employees (local administrators)
- collective farmers

Private entrepreneurs, artisans, shopkeepers, and so on[7]

Szczepanski's model reflects the strong Polish tradition of social respect and prestige for the educated class, the intelligentsia, ranked at the top of the Polish structure. My major objection to that model is that academics, doctors, writers, and artists are listed in the same class as political officials, thus blurring the divide that separated those holding power from the rest of society. Polish political developments in the

1980s revealed once more how important it is for sociologists to grasp that social divide in understanding what was going on in Poland.

The other peculiarity of the model may be found in the peasantry. In Poland, as in Yugoslavia, private agriculture dominated the countryside—a far cry from the Soviet-type of collectivized agriculture. Polish peasants enjoyed much group mobility; in the 1980s, the prosperous ones were eating better, leading a more comfortable life, and even had a higher disposable money income than did some urban workers. On the whole, however, the peasantry was still a deprived group (as indicated by their decline in number and the reluctance of peasant sons to inherit their fathers' businesses), occupying a position at the bottom of the new social hierarchy, as it had under capitalism.

Let us now focus on the question of whether power, so predominant in socialist countries, allowed the monopolization of other resources, such as prestige and income. Many social inquiries found that although power dominated all other resources and could, within broad limits, manipulate the system of stratification itself, it did not always command prestige or esteem; nor did power engender the highest material benefits in society. Best-selling authors, moviemakers, artists, or singers might even earn more money than major party functionaries or cabinet ministers, and only various "perks"—access to special stores, sanatoriums, and "dachas"—might push the latter to the top of the income brackets. The reverse was equally true, one could proceed from the bottom well up the ladders of income, education, and prestige without advancing similarly in terms of power. Of course, there were differences in degree in the relationships among power, prestige, and income in various socialist countries. But Walter Connor concludes that the hierarchy of power, although it dominated, did not subsume the other hierarchies of income and prestige. Connor goes on: "Though the power hierarchy is more dominant in the East than in the West, the design it has imposed leaves some room for achievement and mobility along other dimensions. And there is tension as well between the designs power attempts to impose and the tendency of persons to strive for reward and status and to secure these against the exercise of that power."[8]

As an insider, I should probably add that the organization of power in the East was so pervasive and all-encompassing that its control over citizens was much tighter than in the West, particularly with regard to resources. This generated two contradictory tendencies: on the one hand, those who held power, particularly those at the top, were tempted to acquire equally high positions in terms of prestige by publishing books and gaining reputations as social theorists (a tradition inaugurated by Stalin)—in brief, using power to acquire prestige. On the other hand, too much pressure and control exercised by power over those usually enjoying prestige might serve to increase rather than decrease the social status of the victims. (The case of Andrei Sakharov in the USSR is a very telling illustration of the latter.) Thus, the problem of a socialist society from a social viewpoint is that in its structure the three basic criteria, *power, property* (or income), and *prestige*, intertwined but were not synchronic in establishing a new socialist hierarchy.

LEADERSHIP AND APPARAT

To understand better the social structure and its potential for change, a clear distinction needs to be made between the leadership and the party apparat in communism. As we distinguish between the state system and the leadership that employs the powers of the state in capitalist societies, so must we in socialist countries. Whereas the apparat was trained to follow the general direction of the domestic and foreign policy of the ruling class, the leadership itself had always been the subject of virulent polemics about policies. At times, violent conflicts broke out—as between Stalin and Trotsky or

Bukharin, between Khrushchev and Malenkov, and later between Khrushchev and Brezhnev. In class terms, the apparat corresponds to the Leninist question of *which class holds power*, whereas the political conflict among various factions at the top revolves around the question of *who will exercise power on behalf of the ruling class*: Stalin or Bukharin, the conservatives or the reformers, the moderates or the radicals, the hawks or the doves.

The distinction explains why, on the basis of the general direction of policy, one could fairly predict the position or behavior of the apparat on any given issue. The autonomy enjoyed by the leadership, however, made it difficult to predict which choice or behavior would prevail in the attitude a leader would take in specific events or crises. This was particularly true when a strong leader had succeeded in consolidating his authority. No one was able to predict Stalin's evolution in the late 1920s and early 1930s or his initiative to approach Adolf Hitler and conclude the Molotov-Ribbentrop pact in 1939. Khrushchev was equally unpredictable in his unmasking of Stalin's crimes and in his attempt to place missiles in Cuba.

It is precisely this autonomy of leadership that made significant shifts in policy possible—from Stalin to Khrushchev, from Mao Tse-tung to Deng Xiaoping, from Matyas Rakosi to Janos Kadar, from Antonin Novotny to Alexander Dubček, from Chernenko to Mikhail Gorbachev. Leadership, however, is not an entirely independent variable. We have seen what happened to Khrushchev when his policies came into conflict with the vested interests of the apparat. Even Kosygin's moderate reforms were sabotaged by the apparat and eventually nullified by those in the Politburo who aligned themselves with the apparat. Indeed, the apparat was and acted as a strong conservative force. Therefore, when a new strong leader tried to initiate structural changes that might affect the prerogatives and privileges of the apparat, he was able to carry them out only when a dislocation in the power struc-

ture occurred—a change of guard in the Kremlin, for example, that produced a split of such magnitude in the apparat
that those favoring change got the upper hand. The cases of
Kadar in Hungary (after the 1956 rebellion) and Deng Xiaoping in China (after Mao's death) illustrate the working of
this political dynamic. With Brezhnev's death, the generation
gap in the Soviet Union exploded, enabling Gorbachev to
come to power, although not without hurdles and conflicts.

The generation gap in the USSR appeared as a political
phenomenon as Brezhnev's old guard stubbornly clung to
power, barring newcomers from the Politburo at a time when
the average age in the supreme organ of power was seventy.
Apparently, the old guard feared that the new generation
would think and act differently. And history has confirmed
that suspicion. The new men in the Kremlin led by Gorbachev understood very well that the Soviet Union, a modern
industrial nation, could not be governed in the same fashion
as was post-revolutionary Russia with its archaic agriculture
and mostly illiterate population. The new leaders were com-
mitted to changing Soviet society radically, enabling it to enter the twenty-first century through the front door.

However, the change of guard was not easy. The massive
change in personnel initiated by Gorbachev required a very
long time. The conservative forces, still represented in the
Central Committee, in the ministries, and in the central and
local bureaucracy, were stubbornly resisting change. Even in
the years of president Yeltsin, we have noticed how resilient
are the old political and economic structures created under
the communist system. In the last chapter dealing with the
post-communist society I shall discuss how the party and
state bureaucrats have adapted to the new situation, maintaining fiercely their high social position either politically or
economically.

2

Decline of the Working Class

In October 1986, at a Moscow international scientific conference devoted to the working class in the contemporary world, Soviet party secretary Dobrinin emphasized that the new elements in the situation of the working class in approaching the twenty-first century were related to the scientific-technological revolution. Then he asked: "What are the new social categories within the framework of the working class concept? What is the place that the rapidly expanding category of intellectual workers occupies in the social structure of society? Or of specialists with medium and high skill? How does the numerical growth of the working class correlate with the objective process of social homogenization?"[1] Such questions clearly reveal that there was no scientific definition of the contemporary working class, although this was probably the most important theoretical issue facing scholars and policymakers in the East.

When Karl Marx wrote about basic class relations more than a century ago, he described them as antagonistic and exploitative, implying a clash of interests between capitalists and proletarians, which generated an active class struggle in bourgeois society. In socialist society, however, the capitalist class had been eliminated both economically and politically and, as a result, the exploitative and antagonistic relationship that defined the working class had also gone away. As W. Wesolowski put it: "Deprived of their opposed role, the workers cease to be a class in the traditional sense of the term."[2] They had lost their raison d'être but retained the other characteristics: the workers continued to be tied to a certain type of production (industrial) and a specific type of work (manual); they also possessed specific social and cultural attributes deriving from their new position in society, such as level of income, status in society, social prestige, and class consciousness.

Finally, the relationship to the means of production had been considered by Marx to be the decisive criterion in the differentiation of classes precisely because it determined a certain number of those social attributes. However, in socialist society, the remaining classes had similar relations to the means of production that had been almost completely nationalized, and therefore those relations no longer constituted the decisive criterion in differentiating between classes nor in determining their attributes of social status (income, prestige, life expectancy, and so on). In the 1970s, almost 90% of the population had the same relation to the means of production in most Eastern countries.

This organic destruction of the working class has been compounded by the changes in the work itself brought about by the scientific and technological revolution. Indeed, the technological revolution, and particularly the computer and information devices have changed not only the conditions of material production and the kind of division between mental and manual labor these conditions entail, but also something that goes much deeper, namely the very nature of labor itself. The preponderance of material production is being gradually replaced by information and knowledge. Actually we are now dealing with a transition period from industrialism, which was essentially a system of all kinds of material production, to a post-industrial society in which information and knowledge are becoming dominant factors in the economic process. In this process, manual labor is gradually losing ground, while mental labor takes precedence in industrial enterprises, thus altering the nature of labor.

UNDER CAPITALISM

In the West, this process has resulted in a drastic reduction in the number of industrial workers and a marked increase in information and services jobs. Whereas in 1950, only about 17% of the U.S. work force held information jobs, in the 1990s, over 60% work with information as programmers, teachers, secretaries, lawyers, bankers, and technicians. Only 13% of the labor force is still engaged in manufacturing. Only 5% of the almost 20 million new jobs created in the 1970s were in manufacturing, whereas about 90% were in information, knowledge, or services.[3]

The continuous reduction in the number of industrial workers has become manifest in all advanced capitalist countries. While before World War II, industrial workers in America had represented 70% to 80% of the labor force, in the 1980s their share dropped to 25%. In Germany, their share dropped to 30%. At the October 1986 conference in Moscow, all Western participants noted the same basic trend in the social structure of their countries. The British speaker pointed out that in the British steel industry, the 414,200 employees in 1970 dropped to 143, 200 in 1986; in the shipyards, workers declined from 182,700 to 51,300 in the same period. As a result, the trade unions lost about 4 million members.[4] In Australia, the number of manual workers dropped, in the 1980s, from 49% to 43% of the industrial labor force, whereas the number of intellectual workers increased from 51% to 57%.[5] In France, the number of miners dropped from 500,000 in the 1940s to around 50,000 in the 1980s; railway workers, from 467,000 in 1949 to 219,000 in

1981; and steel workers in Lorraine, from more than 80,000 in 1974 to less than 37,000 in 1983, as reported in *Le Figaro* (January 15, 1990).[6]

Perennial fears that machines will replace man have not been fulfilled up to now. But specialists insist that with microchips, computers, and robots, this may yet happen. One American study conducted at Carnegie-Mellon University asserts that the current generation of robots has the technical capability to perform nearly 7 million existing factory jobs—one-third of all U.S. manufacturing employment. The same study argues that office jobs will be equally affected by automation. Some 38 million out of a total of 50 million existing white-collar jobs may be eliminated by 1990. Xerox Corporation offers a more conservative estimate of 20 to 30 million jobs affected by 1990. Recent studies by the Organization of Economically Developed Countries show that in the mid-1990s the Xerox prediction has been almost entirely confirmed.

UNDER SOCIALISM

Whereas in the West the most characteristic social effect of the technological revolution has been the reduction of manufacturing jobs and the creation of new jobs in services, whereby capitalism is trying to re-establish its equilibrium, in the East the most characteristic social effect of the technological revolution has been the reduction of manual workers and the uprising of intellectuals in both the economy and the society at large. As I have demonstrated in the previous chapter, a continuous differentiation occurs within the industrial workers, with mobility increasing both inside (from unskilled to highly skilled manual workers) and outside, with some of them moving into other social groups of the urban population, particularly as intellectual workers.

In other words, the scientific-technological revolution has widened the scope of the working class, particularly in the direction of its intellectual component, and, as far as we can see, this process is going to continue in the future at an accelerated pace. With science becoming an essential part of the productive forces, the role of the engineers, specialists, and scientists in the industrial process is ever more important—in fact, decisive, in terms of technological progress and economic efficiency. Under the revolution, notes Radovan Richta, the advance of science versus technology and of technology versus production proper becomes a law of development of productive forces. Thus, the development of scientific research may be more important than the expansion of production because the structural transformation in technology, in modernization and rationalization of management, as well as in the development of education and of man in general can have effects much more profound than the construction of factories of existing types and the growth of traditional productive forces.[7]

In the West, American scientist Harvey Brooks reaches the same conclusion: "Economic studies have shown that scientific resources put to good use produce social and economic benefits much greater than investments in physical capital in a modern economy."[8] All these boil down to the upgrading of the human factor. In contrast to the period of industrialization when all the emphasis was on the quantity of capital and labor, today the growth of human forces in terms of quality takes precedence. In short, the scientific-technological revolution marks a period in the history of modern civilization when the most efficient way of increasing the productive forces of society becomes the very development of the human factor, the growing of man's capacities, of his creativity—briefly, the development of man as an end in itself.

In the 1980s, the human factor became a central concept in Soviet sociology. Tatiana Zaslavskaya emphasized that because of the development of the human factor the very object of management was changing. The standards of education, culture, access to information, and legal and personal awareness of the working people attain a higher stage. Their interests and demands become more complex, personality types become more varied. Higher educational standards and cultural development enhance individual tendencies toward an independent status in the factory, an active involvement in decision making, a proper realization of personal creative potentialities. If such cravings are not fulfilled, a person may often become alienated from his work and may be inclined to transfer his interests into other spheres.[9] The logical conclusion is that the new management requires a democratic political environment.

In the famous 1968 Czech study already mentioned dealing with the social impact of the scientific-technological revolution, the authors point out that the attitude of society vis-à-vis scientific knowledge and its capacity or incapacity to put to good use the results of science and of technical innovations has become the infallible criterion of the progressive character of that society. Only the educated cadres, who effectively know the possibilities of modernization today, can make use of science in the contemporary norms of civilization. From a qualitative viewpoint, an incomparably higher level of management and, implicitly, of education is required today than what was once considered sufficient to solve problems of industrialization.[10]

The social conclusion here is that within the working class the center of gravity was shifting from the manual working class to the intellectual one. The 1985 Programme of the Soviet Communist Party acknowledged this: "Revolutionary transformation of the productive forces are leading to an increase in the share of brain work in the activities of the broad mass of workers and collective farm peasants. At the same time, the numerical strength of the intelligentsia is growing and its creative contribution to material production and other spheres of public life is increasing."[11] In the 1980s, in all socialist states, the intelligentsia occupied a position of high social standing in the consciousness of the population, albeit one not yet recognized by officialdom.

Clearly, the manual worker, having brought a tremendous contribution to the construction of socialism, became in the eighties a dwindling social group. In his Report to the 27th Congress, Mikhail Gorbachev said: "Mechanization, automation, computerization . . . must have a clear social orientation. Already in the current five years it is planned to sharply reduce the share of manual labor and, by the year 2000, to bring it down to 15–20%."[12] The statement in the same report that "the working class holds the vanguard place in Soviet society" could have meaning only if the working class concept included the engineers, specialists, and scientists who were the embodiment of the emergent productive forces. Only they, by virtue of their command over socially valued knowledge and expertise, could come to terms with the revolution in computers, information technologies, and global communication.

In China, the 1978 Plenary of the Communist Party's Central Committee changed the social status of intellectuals and publicly acknowledged that intellectuals had become part of the working class. As Deng Xiaoping put it, "The difference between mental laborers and the manual workers lies only in the social division of labor. Those who labor, whether by hand or by brain, are all working people in a socialist society." So, whereas manual workers constituted a social category on the wane, the intellectuals were riding the wave of the future.

Obviously, the working class had been changing its social content for a long time. And yet, the communist parties continued to consider the intellectuals as a social category outside the working class, precisely because they were not prepared to accept the political consequences of a social development that turned the intellectuals into the most advanced and most important part of socialist society. Indeed, the growing role of scientists and engineers in the productive process posed a direct challenge to the party bureaucracy's control over that process: the intellectuals were questioning the right of the party bureaucracy to dispose of the social surplus, which was at the source of its power monopoly.

The analysis of the social structure and the working class in socialism has led this writer to the following conclusions:

1. The scientific-technological revolution had virtually destroyed the notion of the working class as a large, compact sociological unit. Such a class simply no longer existed in social reality. Further, Stalin's simplistic scheme of socialist society (two classes—workers and peasants, and a stratum—the intelligentsia) was equally outdated.

2. The dialectic of social development in socialism was such that before homogenization we witnessed a process of social *differentiation* both in the urban-industrial and in the rural-agricultural environments. This process was widened and accelerated by reform.

    The obtaining socio-occupational groups ranged from unskilled and skilled manual workers to engineers and specialists, white-collar functionaries and state administrative personnel, creative intellectual professions, service employees, private artisans and repairmen, cooperative workers and entrepreneurs, and so on. In the countryside, the notion of peasantry as a class was equally meaningless. An increasing number of mechanizers and repairmen dealing with farm machinery, agronomists, teachers, and administrative personnel had occupations and incomes different from those of ordinary field-workers and peasants. The concept of class was totally inadequate to deal with such diverse and very often conflicting categories. Moreover, the second economy was going to cut across all this. In Hungary, 16% of labor hours and about 40% of personnel income originated from the second economy.

3. The relationship to the means of production, considered by Marx as a decisive criterion in the differentiation of classes, had lost its significance in socialist societies, where about 90% of the means of production belonged to the state. What remained of Lenin's definition of classes was: (a) the place they occupied in social production, (b) their role in the social organization of labor, and (c) the mode of acquisition and share of social wealth of which they disposed. Therefore, the socio-occupational group is a concept much more fertile than class for the study of socialist society. This concept allows for empirical inquiries of

social differentiation in terms of economic status, cultural level, value orientation, and consciousness.

4. The structure of socio-occupational groups in socialist society was determined by *two basic types of division of labor: industrial-agricultural and manual-mental.* It is the division of labor within the two that generated the main social conflicts and contradictions in socialist society.

5. The basic social criteria—power, property (or income), and prestige—intertwined and influenced each other but were not synchronic in establishing a new socialist hierarchy.

THE COMMUNIST REACTION TO THE NEW TECHNOLOGIES

The differentials in wages in the USSR had followed faithfully the vacillations in class policy. In the 1920s when Soviet power began courting the bourgeois engineers and specialists, their wages were set much higher than those of the workers; in the 1960s, the differential reached 48.8% in industry and 55.8% in construction in favor of the engineers and specialists. Under Brezhnev, the policies favoring the manual worker reduced the differential to a mere 10%, and in some industries (construction and machine-tools) the average earnings of workers topped those of engineers.[13]

At the 27th Congress, the egalitarian tendencies in wage policy were sharply criticized. The reform emphasized three principles. First, incomes must be strictly pegged to the performance of the worker; second, highly skilled and highly productive labor should be encouraged for the good of society; and third, while combating unearned income, one must not permit any shadow to fall on those whose honest work was to earn a supplementary income.

At the same Congress, Mikhail Gorbachev stated that the *figure juggling* payment of unearned money, the issue of unmerited bonuses, and the setting of guaranteed pay rates unrelated to the worker's performance was impermissible.

Later, he pointed out that the economic mechanism was geared to average and even poor work, and asked: "How can an economy make progress if it offers hot-house conditions for laggards while hitting front-runners?"[14] An illustration of this is striking. The Omsk amalgamation produced tires of high quality that lasted 50% longer than others; nevertheless, its work collective did not enjoy any benefits whatsoever from producing the best tires in the country.

As for the intersectoral correlation of wages, the *Moscow News* revealed that in the past, "when the national income was distributed, priority was still given to the narrowly understood needs of production"[15]—a wage policy favoring manual workers. The article pointed out that in 1985 the monthly wage of transport workers was 236.6 rubles; in industry, 210.6 rubles. Among cultural workers, it was 117.3 rubles; in health protection, 132.8; and in education, 156. The author concludes that "inside our economic sectors the border has been erased between the wages of people with a special education and without it."[16] The overall effect of such an egalitarian wage system was revealed by a social inquiry mentioned by academician Tatiana Zaslavskaya, who discovered that less than one-third of workers made an effort to do a good job: in the best economic units, 32%; and in those lagging behind, only 17%.[17]

Differentials between various categories of workers were minimal: from unskilled to highly skilled, namely six categories, only 10 to 20 rubles monthly. As a result, workers were not stimulated to raise their professional qualifications. The new wage system initiated in 1987 provided that even within the same category the differential would reach 21% for better performance. Starting from the third category, the worker was now able to earn 24 more rubles monthly for special results. At the same time, poor performers were penalized by earning less than the others.[18] Engineers and highly skilled specialists made a real jump in their earnings. Their average wage could be as high as 80% more than that of workers. Moreover, marked difference was made even within the category of engineers: instead of two scales, four were set: simple engineer, engineer I, engineer II, and principal engineer. The differential between the first and the fourth could reach 130 to 230 rubles monthly in tariff terms (the average industrial wage in 1987 was about 190 rubles). The foreman started from a basic wage of 220 rubles, plus 20% in bonuses; for special performance or innovations, the raise could reach 50%.[19]

The novelty of the new wage system was that the wage fund was no longer to be provided by the national budget. Under the new law adopted by the Supreme Soviet, beginning in 1988 enterprises set pay wages and made determinations about bonuses and other extra pay. Hence, the earnings of the work collective depended on the general performance of the factory, whereas the actual pay of every worker was closely linked to his personal contribution to the factory's profit or loss. In general, incentive possibilities for everybody were dramatically expanded. We are reminded that in Hungary, also, economic reform was accompanied by a sharp differentiation in the wage system. Instead of a 1:3 ratio, the difference between the top and bottom categories increased to 1:9.[20]

Clearly, in the early 1960s—and probably to a larger extent—enterprises started eliminating superfluous labor force in order to become more efficient and profitable. Some economists have estimated that in many industries the redundant labor force was as high as 30% to 40%. One economist had this to say: "The real possibility of losing one's job, of being shifted to a temporary unemployment subsidy, of being forced to move to a new place of employment is not at all bad medicine to cure sloth and drunkenness. Many experts believe it would be cheaper to pay temporary unemployment than to keep on a passel of loafers who can (and do) ruin any efforts to raise efficiency and quality."[21]

Gorbachev pointed out that, in the past, filling vacancies had been the main problem; now the scale on which the excessive work force was trimmed would increase considerably with the speed-up of scientific and technological progress.

Rejecting the idea of unemployment compensation, he warned that such a rearrangement of the work force required close attention and well-considered organizational measures: "We must ensure social guarantees for employment for the working people, for their constitutional right to work. The socialist system has such opportunities."[22]

How did all this affect the differentiation of social classes and strata? Apparently, the main conflicts of interest developed within the working class, between manual workers and intellectuals. To begin with, in a society beset by a scarcity of goods desired by all, their distribution is necessarily such that any increase for one group inevitably reduces the share of the other. With the new differential in wages in favor of engineers, the manual workers saw their share of the cake substantially reduced; although in absolute terms the wage of the latter would remain the same, the soaring income of the engineer would be full of social consequences, affecting social status, prestige, and even life-style. In the new social environment in which the emphasis will be on automation, computer culture, and information technologies, the social gap between the two main strata of the working class was bound to get wider and wider. Furthermore, with enterprises starting to cut redundant labor force, the first to be fired would be the semi-skilled, whereas new automated machines would replace manual workers. The whole aureole surrounding the manual worker would soon wither away.

Therefore, one could hardly expect the stratum of the working class to be exceedingly enthusiastic about *perestroika*. Already the introduction of strict quality control of industrial products had hit those who produced shoddy goods, whereas the measures designed to strengthen order and discipline had struck at loafers and spongers, not to mention the stern anti-drink drive. All in all, such measures made life harder in factories. They were undoubtedly necessary—as steps in the right direction—but this does not mean they were popular.

A bold survey of public opinion undertaken in April 1987 by the new Poll Institute in Moscow on the centerpiece of party policy, *perestroika*, reveals that while 90% of respondents agreed in general with the reform, 50% of workers, asked whether they noticed any changes for the better in Soviet society, answered "not very much"; 62% of workers thought that the only result of *perestroika* thus far was more work; and 45% were skeptical that it would affect their lives. The only category that thought significant changes had taken place was the intelligentsia: 85%.[23]

In early November 1987, Gorbachev noted "a certain increase in the resistance of conservative forces that see *perestroika* simply as a threat to their selfish interests and objectives." He emphasized that "this resistance can be felt not only at management level, but also in work collectives." With regard to management level, he went on, some 18 million people were employed in administration, 2.5 million in the apparatus of administrative and law enforcement bodies, and some 15 million in the managing bodies of associations, enterprises, and organizations. All this amounted to 15% of the country's manpower.[24] The leading Soviet economist Abel Aganbeyan had noted that "a 30% to 50% reduction in administrative personnel could be made by the end of December 1987, with 4% of those administrators retiring and the rest being relocated."

In the countryside also, Soviet sociologists noted a process of social differentiation, and at least four main occupational groups were recognized as statistical entities: administrative personnel and specialists, mechanizers (or agricultural machinery operators), poultry and livestock farmers or handlers, and ordinary field workers. In addition to these four main groups, frequent reference was made in official and unofficial sources to a number of other groups without which Soviet agriculture would not have been able to function at all, such as builders, service personnel, and a variety of rustic handymen, not to mention the 4 to 5 million able-bodied peasants who in the 1960s and 1970s had been engaged exclusively in tending private plots and whose number was now substantially greater. The differential in income between the top and bottom of the occupation hierarchy was significant.

M. F. Kovaleva's inquiry was made in the Amur oblast, but other studies speak of a more general scale of earnings in collective farms extending from 100 to 250 new rubles. K. A. Shabeikov, writing in 1963, mentioned situations where chairmen's earnings were 15 to 19 times higher than those of field workers on their farms.[25] According to rates recommended in All-Union legislation, vice chairmen were entitled to up to 90% of the chairmen's earnings and other responsible administrators and specialists received 60% to 90%, in descending order of skill. The service personnel were apparently the lowest paid people on the farm. In 1966, for example, the basic earnings varied from 70 rubles a month for those in cultural and educational institutions down to 40 rubles for watchmen and cleaners.[26]

Later decisions extending the private plots or renting (or leasing) farmland to individual peasants, families, and cooperatives for up to fifty years were bound to accentuate social differentiation in the countryside. Moreover, the decision to allow individual peasants privately to buy tractors, trucks, and other equipment previously considered "means of production" available only to the socialist sector and to hire workers created entirely new socio-occupational groups with interests different from those working in a *kolkhoz* or state farm. The process of social differentiation in both urban and rural areas and, in particular, the resulting growing disparities in income among socio-occupational groups reopened the debate on equality in socialist society.

THE ODYSSEY OF THE MANUAL WORKER

Throughout Eastern Europe the drive for industrialization brought about significant changes in the social structure. As in the USSR, the main direction of the social mobility process was from the peasantry to the industrial working class as well as from both these social classes into groups of local and central party bureaucrats of state executives and of intellectuals. Particularly in the early phase of industrialization—namely, from 1950 to 1960—the number of people moving from agriculture into cities increased in Albania by 145%, in Bulgaria by 120%, in Romania by 53%, in Poland by 46%, and in Hungary by 49%.[27] Of course, the process was much slower in Czechoslovakia and East Germany.

Few statistics are available in the East. In Poland, where a strong sociological team had already taken shape in the 1960s, a survey was conducted in 1969 on the social mobility of the People's Councils, the elected organs of local government. The survey revealed that over 90% of the permanent members of People's Councils' executive bodies came from worker and peasant families.[28] Another study by the Polish Academy of Science in 1964 found that 60.6% of all managers of socialized industrial plants came from workers' families; 18.6%, from those of peasant origin; 17.8%, from non-manual workers' families; and 3% from other groups.[29]

The village-to-city migration process raises many sociological problems that have not been much studied. First, in many Eastern European countries, unlike in Russia of 1917, there was a rather large class of proletarians in the wake of World War II. Especially in Czechoslovakia in the early 1930s, the share of those employed in industry was as high as 38%; in Hungary, 24%; in Poland, 19.4%; and in Romania, Bulgaria, and Yugoslavia, only 8 to 10%. But the proletarian core was quickly reduced to the size of a drop in the peasant sea flooding into cities the moment socialist industrialization took over. Nevertheless, one must take into account that in pre-war Eastern Europe the few workers who were needed in the incipient industrial factories were relatively skilled, and therefore their pay and standard of living were relatively high—at that time, not much lower than in Western Europe. Therefore, the relatively meager group of pre-war industrial workers who remained in the factories after the revolution suffered in fact a deterioration of their living standards in most Eastern European countries when the policy of depressed wages came into effect. Even in Russia, as revealed so daringly by the Soviet scholar O. I. Shkaratan, in the wake of the revolution the real income of workers fell by 9.6% from its pre-revolutionary size, and even after industrialization was launched, the income of that group remained lower than it had been in October 1917.

Initially, those workers did not protest that loss because revolutionary fervor was very strong. Later, they could not do anything about their wages being dissolved in the vast mass of peasant emigrants joining the industrial labor force. For all those newcomers, the living conditions in the cities meant a substantial improvement. The urban environment, with all its deficiencies in terms of housing and food, was incomparably better than anything they had experienced in the countryside. The job security they enjoyed by entering the factory, the wide opportunities opened before them in social mobility, health care, education, and the fresh experience of urban shopping—all these transformed the new working class not only into loyal supporters of the new order of things, but also into a social group with important vested interests in its continuation and stability. One author, commenting on this social phenomenon, rightly concludes: "One cannot properly understand the working of the web of socialist governments in Eastern Europe without trying to comprehend the different meaning of the political culture associated with the understanding of this group's sense of achievement and personal indebtedness to the victorious revolution."[30]

What made the manual worker, of peasant extraction, the social hero in Eastern Europe was not only his readiness to accept the depressed wage system that was required by the accumulation policy for industrialization. It was his particular political culture that was to the liking of Stalinist and neo-Stalinist regimes. Centuries of exclusion from political life induced such a worker never to think of political expression as something that could help him find a solution to his troubles. Neither was freedom of the press a dream of illiterates. And, of course, village tradition had not been conducive to feeling the need for freedom of organization. Rather, the cozy security of a closed integrated community was what they brought with them into factory life. Even the spontaneous suspicion of intellectuals, so often a feeling among the workers of peasant extraction, was something that Eastern leaders came to appreciate and sometimes to exploit politically.

To sum up: *the manual worker of peasant origin was the ideal social base for the Communist Party as molded by Stalin.* Incapable of exercising power himself in a modern industrial society, the manual worker made it necessary for a "vanguard" to exercise power on his behalf. His political culture made him the perfect object of the "revolution from the above." In its turn, the fact that the regime was based on, and devoted to, the true industrial worker who was building socialism with his own hands constituted an impeccable ideological credential for the party bureaucracy to prove its political legitimacy. In 1967, the Stalinist leader of Czechoslovakia, Antonin Novotny, before being deposed by the new reformist leadership, appealed for help from the workers. In 1970 in Poland, leader Wladyslaw Gomulka, when told that he was deposed, also wanted to call a meeting to address the workers: he was convinced they would help him.

However, as mentioned earlier, the fundamental condition necessary to keep the loyalty and support of industrial workers was to ensure continuous improvement of their standard of living. From the moment that promise (so many times reiterated in party documents) was broken, the party was in trouble. It was the working class—and, in particular, the shipyard workers in Gdansk, Gdynia, Slupsk, and Szczeczin—who in December 1970 went on strike against the government's decision to increase the price of food and services with a simultaneous wage freeze. Learning from that experience, the Hungarian government, before deciding on a drastic restructuring of food prices, consulted the union leadership; the latter suggested as compensation a 20% raise in wages, which in turn required the government to cut investments. This procedure may well explain why the painful increases in food prices were accepted by the Hungarian workers.

Brezhnev's predilection for industrial workers made him formulate a series of measures designed to maintain the social status and role of that class in Soviet society at a time when the scientific-technological revolution began to threaten them. One of the most important measures in that direction was in the domain of education. Noting the increasing number of students in higher education (universities and polytechnic institutions)—from 12,000 in 1940 to 3,860,000 in 1965 and 4,854,000 in 1975—Brezhnev decided to offer fifteen-year-old pupils, after eight-year school, an alternative to the general-school-leading-to-university, namely a technical school with a two- or three-year course set up to train skilled workers for factories and agriculture. As a result, 47.3% of pupils in 1981–1982 were attending technical or vocational schools.

In 1977, the Soviet minister of education, M. A. Prokofiev, emphasized that historically speaking, a high level of education predetermined the training of people for the sphere of intellectual labor. Now it is necessary to destroy these notions. In the conditions of compulsory secondary education for all, the school must prepare its pupils in the university, *technikum*, and vocational school, and for working directly in the factory or on the *kolkhoz*.[31]

Brezhnev was equally alerted by trends in the composition of the Communist Party. In 1966 the percentage of intellectuals in party membership increased to 35.6; in 1971, to 41.1; and in 1977, intellectuals became the largest social group in the party, at 51.3%. A a result, under Brezhnev a determined effort was made to draw workers into the party, to prevent an imbalance favoring the intelligentsia. Brezhnev began to speak about the "proletarization of the party." The political portrait of the Brezhnev era painted by Mikhail Gorbachev ("conservative sentiments, inertia, a tendency to brush aside everything that did not fit into conventional patterns, and an unwillingness to come to grips with outstanding socio-economic questions")[32] was fairly accurate in describing the consolidation of the Soviet class structure in the 1970s. The central actor of that class structure was *the manual worker*, and it was only natural that a policy designed to maintain the manual worker's position of pre-eminence in Soviet society should come into conflict with technological process and innovation.

The most striking facet of that policy is revealed by the wage system of the 1970s. Russian official statements in Moscow noted that while in 1965, at the time of the reform in progress, the differential in wages between workers and specialists (chiefly engineers) had risen to 46%, the differential in the late 1970s and early 1980s dropped to a mere 10%. In addition, in the construction industry and in machine-tool industries, the average worker's wage became higher than that of engineers.[33] Academician Tatiana Zaslavskaya related that many engineers renounced their positions to become workers,[34] and *Literaturnaya Gazeta*, in May 1987, mentioned several cases where engineers earning about 200 rubles a month took jobs as skilled workers and earned 250 to 260 rubles a month.

In spite of the paucity of statistics on income published in the 1970s, some of the existing studies clearly show that the ratio of earnings of engineering-technical workers to earnings of manual workers dropped substantially in the Brezhnev era.[35] In 1979, engineers and specialists earned less than one-fifth more than workers in industry and a mere 4.3% more than those in construction.

Even in Czechoslovakia the underestimation of intellectuals was apparent. In 1962, only 25% of managers and technical cadres in economic enterprises had university diplomas; in state administration, only 29% of those occupying executive positions were college graduates; and even in research and development institutions, only 3.7% of employees had scientific training—a social policy in striking contrast to the level of education in Czechoslovakia, as pointed out by Czech author Radovan Richta.[36] The advocates of reform frequently criticized the egalitarian income structure and argued in favor of higher rewards for the qualified personnel so essential in the modernization of the economy. Ota Sik observed that "over the years, and particularly since 1959, there occurred an increasingly damaging leveling of wages, which in turn had a harmful effect on progress in science and technology."[37]

Given the aims of the reform, it is not surprising that the opponents of reform tended to represent themselves as defenders of the working class, denouncing Ota Sik as an advocate of capitalist economies. Antonin Novotny and his associates turned to the industrial workers for support against the intelligentsia. In retrospect, it seems fair to assume that one of the reasons why the Czechoslovak workers did not actively oppose the Soviet invasion and the Gustav Husak regime was precisely their perception of the reform as a threat to their interests. In fact, the reformers themselves acknowledged that egalitarianism had enjoyed "broad domestic working class support" and that under the Novotny government "these classes had achieved their goal—truly unique egalitarianism in the wage sector."[38]

Some Western observers have drawn attention to the "anti-labor overtones" of the intellectuals' campaign and to the "class bias" implicit in some proposals for reform. Actually, even before the Prague Spring, the pressure of qualified white-collar forces for a sharper differential in their favor began to assert itself, influencing the wage policy of the regime. Of course, the Husak regime in Czechoslovakia also restored the previous "social correlation of forces," improving the relative position of the manual worker. The average wage of the industrial worker in 1980 (2,723 krone) was very close to that of the scientist (2,987), and that of a construction worker (2,983) almost equaled that of a scientist.

In Poland, where before World War II nearly all intellectuals had earned more than manual workers, under socialism the wage policy favored an equalization of income between the two social strata. In the middle of the income bracket table in 1963 (from 1,200 to 2,000 zlotys), comprising about 40% of the industrial labor force, both manual workers and engineers earned the same amount of money. In the income brackets higher than 2,000 zlotys, manual workers earned 33.1% whereas engineers and specialists accounted for 40.8%, which shows that even in the highest brackets the difference between the two was minimal. The conclusion was that the less skilled were overpaid and the party and state bureaucrats were even more so.[39]

During the five-year plans from 1970 to 1985, when official rhetoric in the East was proclaiming the urgency of assimilating the scientific-technological revolution, the actual wage policy was still favoring the manual worker. As figures for engineers and specialists in industry are not available, we are comprising the average wages of the latter with those of the technocrats. Invariably, the 1985 average wage of workers in industry and construction topped that of scientists, professors, and creative intellectuals in all Eastern countries. In only two socialist countries, Bulgaria and Czechoslovakia, was the average wage of scientists slightly higher than that of manual workers. It is very significant that the same relationship between the two categories (manual workers versus intellectuals) had been stubbornly maintained for over fifteen years in all the socialist countries.

In a country such as Poland, where sociologists found a strong tradition of social respect and prestige for the intelligentsia, who were considered to have been the guardians of national unity and conscience, such wage policy evidently ran not only against the technological revolution but also against deep-seated national values. One social inquiry revealed an apparent incongruence between the way people viewed the place of a social category on the scale of social prestige and the amount of its income as decided by party policy. A teacher in Poland, who earned between 1,500 and 2,000 zlotys per months, and a nurse, who earned about 1,500 zlotys, occupied higher places on the scale of prestige than a turner, who made 3,000 to 4,000 zlotys a month.[40]

But the extreme form of that class policy was to be found in Romania. From 1965 to 1971 we witnessed a Khrushchev-type phase, with political openings heralding a relaxation of authoritarian methods, criticism of one-man rule, and praise of collective leadership that coincided with a cultural thaw and condemnation of administrative interference with the arts. The climax came with Ceausescu's public disapproval of the 1968 Soviet military intervention in Czechoslovakia. Conversely, from 1971 to December 1989, a Brezhnev-type phase was in place, with the manual worker exalted as social hero, a much harsher one-man rule, and a conservative backlash in culture and arts.

The anti-intellectual policy was applied on a scale larger than anywhere else in the East—from wage policy to the whole gamut of education and scientific and artistic activities. An engineer with ten years of experience and specialization in machines with digital control in Britain earned 3,500 lei monthly; another, with specialization in optical instruments in Japan, earned 3,300 lei monthly, whereas the average wage of the worker in the coal, oil, and machine-tool industries was 4,000 lei monthly. State measures designed to downgrade or reduce cultural activities were instituted one after another. First came a decision to annul the special stipend for the members of the Academy that had been granted to free leading scientists from the daily material worries. Then royalties for books and scientific articles were drastically reduced. State subsidies for the arts were cut to the bone. Subsidies for theaters dropped from 70% to 30%; similar reductions occurred for filmmaking, operas, symphonic orchestras, and buying paintings. The number of students declined from year to year (181,200 in 1982; 174,000 in 1983; 166,300 in 1984, and 159,800 in 1985); from 1985 to 1989, not one classroom was built. In striking contrast to the official rhetoric extolling the virtues of the scientific-technological revolution (even a five-year plan was baptized as such), all sources of information about its development were effectively closed, from access to foreign journals and books to participation of Romanian scientists and engineers in international conferences and seminars. In short, a policy designed to freeze the existing economic, social, and political structures was in force in Romania.

Typical of such a highly centralized form of power was the control of every means of production, allowing no significant part of the productive activity or economic initiative to be in the hands of individuals, so that no segment of society could be independent of the state. In Romania, even private peasants and individual households were subject to state plan regulations. Forms of life that stubbornly resisted the impact of the system—such as familial, emotional, and sexual relationships—were also under strong pressure to conform to official values and rules. Actually, in all communist economy countries the differential between manual workers and the intelligentsia was continuously reduced in the 1960s and early 1970s. In Romania, the difference was the most extreme.

WHERE THE MARKET SQUEEZED IN

To explore the changes in the social structure brought about by the introduction of market mechanisms in a socialist economy, the most telling case is that of Yugoslavia. Immediately after World War II, as a result of sweeping changes in the economic infrastructure, the social and material power of the bourgeoisie and rentier classes was stripped away. Industrial and commercial enterprises were nationalized, although small shops and handicrafts for the most part were left in private ownership. About four million acres of land, much of it belonging to the Catholic Church, the banks, and the *Volkdeutsche* (ethnic Germans) were expropriated by the state; about half of it was redistributed to the peasants. As a result, the class structure of Yugoslavia followed the patterns common to the other Eastern European countries. Income distribution showed a highly egalitarian trend, with average earnings of engineers and specialists in the late 1940s exceeding those of manual workers by only 25%. Food was rationed in accordance with the physical demands of an individual's occupation, favoring manual workers over sedentary white-collar employees.

Beginning in the early 1950s, after Yugoslavia's break with the Eastern bloc, a series of reforms were set in motion that would turn social processes in a different direction. The extent of central control over the economy was substantially reduced, and a limited system of worker self-management was introduced. Nevertheless, sociologists found that, far from following the social patterns prevailing the West, the class structure and the overall distribution of rewards in Yugoslavia were closer to those of Eastern Europe. Here, I should recall an important theoretical point made by Charles Bettelheim, who rejected the idea that the market is an impelling force leading toward the restoration of capitalism: "In reality this is not so. Everything depends on the manner in which it [plan or market] is dealt with, and this manner depends on class relations, including those at the ideological level."[41]

In a study of Yugoslavia's reform, the author notes that the main "break" in the stratification system occurred within the working class, epitomizing once again that in a socialist society intraclass differences become more significant than interclass ones. Thus, one of the consequences of the reform carried out in Yugoslavia over two decades was the gradual erosion of the egalitarian income structure of the 1940s. The release of market forces had produced a steady drift toward increasing income differentials favoring, in particular, the highly skilled and qualified groups. Whereas in 1951, highly qualified white-collar workers were earning only about 25% more than unskilled workers, by 1961 they were getting three and a third times more. Also, skilled workers made rapid gains, consolidating their advantage over both unskilled workers and office workers. It is interesting that unemployment resulting from a more competitive economic environment was striking at the manual worker, while engineers and specialists were able to manage the situation better.[42]

However, when it came to positions of authority in industry, the correlation of forces looked different, reflecting the basic political fact that in Yugoslavia the regime also relied chiefly on the manual workers. The ideological bias in favor of the industrial worker was reflected in the legal stipulation that manual employees must occupy at least 75% of the seats on workers' councils. In the Yugoslav system, workers' councils enjoyed important prerogatives: they were responsible for the hiring of all employees, including white-collar workers and technicians; they held ultimate authority over the dismissal of workers; and they had a say in the allocation of jobs within the plant, in setting production norms and wage rates for piece-work, in the distribution of bonuses, and the like. True, it was the skilled manual worker who dominated the workers' councils, whereas semi-skilled and unskilled workers were poorly represented. In second place on the councils were the highly qualified white-collar employees.[43]

Another study found that the great majority of communists serving on these councils were skilled manual workers, and less than 12% were semi-skilled and unskilled. The author concludes: "There is thus a strong association between the labor aristocracy, the Communist Party and the workers' councils, sufficient at least to support a generalized image of 'them' in the eyes of unskilled laborers."[44]

Interestingly, sociologist Frank Parkin claims that the occupational group ranking highest in material and status terms, as a result of market forces, was the white-collar intelligentsia. Those in the most important technical, creative, administrative, and professional positions in society enjoyed certain kinds of privileges and advantages that gave them a more favorable status, as compared to other groups, than was indicated by income differentials alone. Thus, the intelligentsia generally had greater access than other groups to high-quality accommodations, official cars and other state property, foreign currency for trips abroad, and other "perks."[45]

There was in Yugoslav society a certain incongruence between the political class holding power (and its social policy) and the evolution of class forces in society, the former relying chiefly on the manual workers, whereas the latter was pushing the technical and creative intelligentsia upward. In philosophical terms, the first is mainly ideologically motivated and the latter is more of an objective phenomenon.

An important theoretical point arising from the above mentioned studies is that to put together the intelligentsia engaged in various economic and social activities with those holding administrative jobs is to ignore the fundamental difference made by a position of power in society, a position that sets the latter category apart from the rest of society. Essentially, the same mistake is to be found in books maintaining that the intellectuals in socialist countries already constituted the social class now holding power in those countries: "If there is a new dominant class in Eastern Europe it has been composed since the sixties at least of the intelligentsia as a whole rather than just the bureaucracy narrowly defined," argue two Hungarian authors.[46] We could then ask two legitimate questions: First, if the intellectuals were the class in power during the 1970s, why did they formulate and implement a policy that in every respect, starting with wages, favored manual workers while denying engineers, specialists, and scientists the payment and role in society commensurate with their decisive contribution to the progress of the country?[47] Second, if the intellectuals were the class in power in Hungary, why did the two authors leave the country?

Statistics show that in Hungary, precisely in the 1960s, when the authors claim that the intellectuals had become the dominant class, the wages and earnings of the technical intelligentsia began to drop. For the first time in history, a dominant class initiated a wage policy that went against its members, if we are to accept the conclusion of the book.

Interestingly, the issue also divides Western ideologists. One author finds a growing "schism between party members increasingly drawn from the intelligentsia and the party elite, who are full-time officials."[48] Another author goes even further, arguing that the "key antagonism" in socialist society is between the political and administrative apparatus of the state, which gives effective legal guardianship of socialized property, and those groups (the intelligentsia) whose social power inheres in its command of the skills, knowledge, and general attributes that are held to be of central importance to productive and scientific development in modern society.[49] On the other hand, a political sociologist finds that intellectuals have an extremely high rate of party membership and that institutional arrangements under state socialism involve the relatively very effective incorporation of the intelligentsia into institutions of the state. On that basis, he concludes: "The intelligentsia has to be clearly situated in the context of the state apparatus." Of course, the whole strategy of development and modernization initiated by state socialism requires the skills and knowledge of the intelligentsia, and therefore a major effort was made to integrate this class into the state apparatus.[50] However, state socialism is politically and ideologically devoted to the manual worker, and as such it comes into conflict with the intelligentsia. Therefore, intellectuals are integrated into the state apparatus only to the extent that they betray their class, accepting the official ideology that worships the industrial worker as the dominant social factor in socialist society.

To sum up: A clear distinction should be made between the social structure and the political class in power, as well as between the individual belonging to a social class or stratum and the individual occupying an executive position in the government. A worker laboring in a factory is completely distinct from a worker becoming a local party secretary or a member of the cabinet. The same holds true for an engineer in a mine as opposed to an individual who becomes a minister. In fact, this is what this chapter is all about.

THE POLITICAL VERDICT OF SOCIAL DIFFERENTIATION

The evolution of social classes and strata in the socialist countries has a direct bearing on the role and function of the Communist Party. Even its basic conception and structure were bound to be affected by the social differentiation taking place in socialist society. The Communist Party was initially conceived of as the political party of the working class, by which Lenin meant the industrial proletariat doing manual work. The monolithic conception of the party was based on the assumption of a large, compact working class sufficiently integrated and homogeneous to account for a common ideological consciousness and a set of common material and cultural interests. Of course, as the party of the future, the Communist Party was supposed to lead a working class that would be growing numerically and acquiring an ever more important role in industrial society.

Today, all these assumptions have proven to be outdated, *dépassées*. As documented earlier, the scientific-technological revolution has virtually destroyed the notion of the working class as a large, compact sociological unity: the manual workers constitute a waning social category in terms of number, social status, and prestige. Intraclass differences and, in particular, socio-occupational groups within the working class are becoming more diverse and articulate, ranging from unskilled manual workers to white-collar employees, engineers and specialists, managerial cadres, and so on. The ongoing reform can be expected to widen and accelerate the process of social differentiation within existing classes and create new social groups outside them. For one thing, the private sector, especially in services, will grow substantially and so will the social group taking shape on that basis.

A very interesting seminar took place in May 1988 in Novosibirsk, Russia, which, for the first time, rather candidly discussed the issue: *Perestroika, kto za, kto protiv?* (Who is in favor and who is against *perestroika?*). The seminar examined the findings of a group of economists and sociologists led by Tatiana Zaslavskaya, who for six years had conducted research on the Soviet social structure and the position of various social groups with respect to reform:

1. Manual workers engaged in preindustrial work and the elements *déclassés* are against *perestroika* (economically and politically).
2. The skilled workers support the democratization process but hesitate on economic changes.
3. Highly qualified specialists and those engaged in creative activities are in favor of both democratization and economic reform.
4. Leaders at the top are also in favor of both.
5. The administrative apparatus and economic and state bureaucrats oppose reforms (political and economic).
6. Managers of enterprises support economic reform but not political reform.[51]

Based on these findings, the seminar raised the following questions: How will these positions of major social groups be reflected in the Communist Party? Where and how will they be able to defend their interests and express their views?

In both the Soviet Union and China, it was only natural that the kind of positions defined by the Novosibirsk seminar should be reflected in the only political party that existed.

Therefore, the social groups mentioned above had to be given a chance to come out of hiding and openly express their views. Socialist society had reached a stage of development in which the level of education and political experience made its social groups aware of their specific interests and ready to define them actively. In a socially differentiated society, political pluralism is a *must* if violent social eruptions and clashes are to be avoided and economic activities are to follow an ascending line.

The Communist Party, facing social conditions that had not been anticipated by its founders, was going through a crisis. The question was whether the Communist Party would be able to reshape its conception and structure so as to absorb and accommodate, in the political sphere, the various interests of the social groups existing or taking shape in a socialist society, particularly those of the most advanced group of that society, the intellectuals.

Mikhail Gorbachev quite often mentioned "socialist pluralism." Zhao Ziyang, at the Chinese Party Congress in 1987, suggested that the Trade Unions, Communist Youth League, Women's Federation, and other mass organizations should be allowed "to better express and defend the specific interests of the masses they represent," emphasizing, of course, that all such activities would take place under the leadership of the Communist Party.[52] This was a first step toward pluralism in Chinese society.

But what about the Communist Party itself? The point was that to democratize socialist society and make it pluralistic, one had to democratize the Communist Party first. In other words, one must touch the very core of the power structure if political reform is to be *real.* After all what is socialist pluralism?

To begin with, there are only two possible types of political pluralism: a multi-party system or pluralism within a one-party system. From the viewpoint of political science, the communist system can be characterized as nonrepresentative, bureaucratic, and therefore repressive. It lacks flexibility in adapting to new situations and has an error-prone decision-making process. It is a system that lacks any feedback mechanism; in other words, it has no way of correcting its mistakes. Even proposals meant to improve its functioning and performance were not discussed publicly. But its principal historical fault lies in its status quo inclination—its resistance to change and progress—which makes for probably the greatest paradox in history, this being a party that was supposed to lead the march into the future.

Party pluralism means renouncing the monolithic conceptions of the Communist Party and transforming it into a political organization representative of all social classes and major groups. The peasantry and the intellectuals had never been properly represented in the Bolshevik Party—a fact that allowed the forced collectivization, mass deportation, and killings of peasants, as well as the massive repression of the intelligentsia, to be carried out without any effective resistance from within the party. If it is to have political legitimacy, the one-party system must guarantee all the component social forces it claims to represent and provide its members every opportunity to defend their specific interests and to express their different views. Otherwise, the emergence of alternative political parties is inevitable and perfectly legitimate.

The 1921 resolution prohibiting factions in the Bolshevik Party had the effect of restricting debate on policy issues within the party, thereby suppressing inner-party democracy. As a result, the party was run by an oligarchic bureaucracy that made decisions without consultations of party members—what Stalin cynically referred to as a "military democracy," meaning that party members were merely expected to carry out orders from above. Although Stalin's brutal methods and excesses were eliminated, military discipline and the interdiction to express dissenting views remained in force.

Tolerance of diverse groups and factions within the Communist Party was viewed by reformist leaders as the hallmark of party democracy, and democracy in socialist society begins with democracy in the party. In a one-party system, the Communist Party can function as the leading political force in society only if it offers the constituent parts of that society the full opportunity to express their views. In fact, however, from the time when factions were formally proscribed, one faction—whether it was Stalin's, Khrushchev's or Brezhnev's—invariably ran the party by eliminating all others. This held true for China, too, where Mao, in an effort to impose his own policies, eliminated Liu Shao Tsi and twice demoted Deng Xiaoping. Innumerable are the names of brave and honest communist leaders who were executed in the name of the dreadful monolithic conception. The interdiction of factions at times even brought the law of the jungle to communist parties, as was tragically illustrated by the Grenada experience, in which one faction murdered the leader of another.

What were the main arguments in favor of monolithism? In 1921, at the Tenth Congress of the Bolshevik Party, Lenin introduced the resolution abolishing factions as a *temporary* measure dictated by the gravity of the situation in Soviet Russia. He insisted, however, that the rights of minority views in the party should be strictly observed. Under his leadership, the party's democratic norms were somewhat respected and clashing views were tolerated. Those who opposed Lenin's decisions or criticized his policies were not penalized. Lev Kamenev and Grigori Zinoviev, who voted against the decision to start the revolution in October 1917, remained members of the Politburo, as did those who opposed the Brest-Litovsk peace treaty with Germany. Actually, Lenin was twice in a minority position in the Central Committee.

The tolerance of clashing views in party life continued even after Lenin's death. In the 1920s and even in the early 1930s opposite platforms and programs clashed in the party and in the public and were presented at party congresses, leading one of the most vitriolic of Western historians of the

Soviet Communist Party to characterize that period as "the golden era of Marxist thought."[53] Bukharin was the chief editor of *Pravda*, and the fact is that his alternative strategy to Stalin's, which enjoyed the support of Aleksey Rykov (premier) and Mikhail Tomsky (chairman of the trade unions), was predominant for almost a decade in the party. In general, the Bolshevik Party, up to 1938, was more diverse and much more vivid politically and ideologically than at any other subsequent period in Soviet history—to this day.

Therefore, the argument that factions may divide the party and make it inept to lead and govern is erroneous. Historical experience shows that the existence of factions did not impair the capacity of the Bolshevik Party to carry out the revolution successfully, to defeat the White generals and the foreign intervention, to overcome the capitalist encirclement and to start building the economy and reconstruct the country after a devastating civil war. If under adverse conditions—domestic and international—factions did not negatively affect the party's capacity to govern, why should they later, after such conditions had all but disappeared?

As for democratic centralism, historical experience shows that it was merely centralism, bureaucratic centralism, with its democratic component totally missing. No political initiative from below, from party members, surfaced in the party. All political initiative was concentrated at the top. No alternative programs or platforms were presented at party congresses or conferences or were discussed in the party. One single program, one single solution to a problem was being set forth by the party leader. Thus, the outcome of the deliberations was predetermined: no alternative solutions had a chance, no critical analysis took place, no arguments clashed: the course of action was already decided. I reread all the verbatim record of post-war party congresses, including that of 1986, and could not find one speaker taking issue with the party leader's report. Classic was Khrushchev's fantastic program to build a communist society and overtake America by 1980, which was *unanimously* adopted by the 1961 congress. Clearly, such a decision-making mechanism is anti-scientific and error-prone.

In the Gorbachev days, some theoreticians argued that the legalization of groups and factions within the party would set the mechanism right. The debate would be *real* with different and even conflicting views clashing. The general secretary would speak at the end of such debates, after listening to various opinions and consulting the other members of the Politburo.

The basic question remains: Was such a radical change of the Communist Party possible? I think not. Actually, in all the Eastern European countries a multi-party political system has been established and reinforced by free elections. Even the leader of the Communist Party of Russia, Gennady Zyuganov, has publicly declared his support for the multi-party system in Russia. The issue still remains in China.

3

The New Social Structure after 1989

The events in 1989 in Eastern Europe are considered a *revolution* because of the *structural changes* that followed not only in the political sphere (the multi-party system and democratic freedoms) and in the economic one (the transition to a market economy), but also in the *social* sphere. However, although many studies have been published on the political and economic changes in the region, no comprehensive analysis has been undertaken with regard to the profound changes in social relations.

Of course, we are confronted in this case with a situation without precedent in the history of social formations. The painstaking journey we in Eastern Europe made from capitalism to socialism, totally unprepared and ill-inspired, ended in a complete failure, so we must now go back to where we started. In terms of politics and economics, we may to some extent be advised and chaperoned by the West on the road to capitalism and democracy; however, the transition in the social sphere is carried out from below, abruptly and spontaneously, without any planning.

1990 AND 1991: THE OLD STRUCTURE SURVIVES

At the beginning, the social transformations in Romania were marked by a different speed from those in Poland, Hungary, and Czechoslovakia. The very character of the revolution was different. On December 21, 1989, the whole world watched on television that unforgettable scene: in Bucharest, the dictator Ceausescu stood on the balcony of the Central Committee building, visibly perplexed by the unprecedented rumble of boos and catcalls pervading the 100,000-strong crowd assembled in the vast Palace Square. One who never experienced the ritual of the huge but perfectly organized mass meetings so carefully staged during the Ceausescu era cannot fully appreciate the significance of that fantastic scene marked by Ceausescu's bewildered, haggard look. What followed that evening and the following days was a popular explosion that was met by the tyrant's order to his loyalist forces to shoot into the rioting crowds. The whole week was beset by military clashes, urban guerilla warfare, destructions, and killings.

Why was Romania's revolution the only violent one in Eastern Europe? In Poland, Hungary, and Czechoslovakia two political factors—a reformist wing in the Communist Party and an organized opposition outside the party—struck a deal that facilitated the peaceful transition of power and the formation of a center-right government. Not so in Romania. The Ceausescu dictatorship was so brutal and effective that no reformist group could take shape within the party; nor could opposition forces organize themselves. As a result, a center-left group took hold of power, dominated by a hard core of dissident communists.

In retrospect, the predominance of ex-communists in the new power structure did not prove to be the right political solution. Ceausescu's pathology extended even after his death. As the historical task of the new regime was the restoration of capitalism, the proper political force to carry out such a profound social transformation would have been a *center-right* government comprised of people who sincerely believed in the merits of capitalism. This was the case in Poland, Hungary, and Czechoslovakia. In Romania, however, the electorate did not share the political logic and confirmed in power the center-left government in the May 1990 elections. President Iliescu got 85% of the popular vote and his party, the National Salvation Front, got 67%. Consequently, in 1990 and 1991, nothing happened sufficiently strong to shake up the old social structure simplistically defined by Stalin's triptych (two classes—workers and peasants, plus a stratum—the intellectuals).

With a labor force of 40% workers, 28% to 29% peasants, and less than 20% employed in services, Romania qualified as an underdeveloped nation in European terms, and the National Salvation Front became the political beneficiary of that status. Actually, the NSF inherited the social base of the Communist Party, which Ceausescu had deceived and alienated. The NSF courted and pampered the industrial workers with a five-day work week and higher wages, in sharp contrast with the decline of production and productivity.

The peasants got 30% of the arable land as individual plots and the freedom to produce and sell their output without restrictions—a far cry from Ceausescu's harsh policy enforced with the help of militia. As seen in Table 1, the number of industrial workers remained almost the same. Nor were there significant changes in the countryside. Some minor movements occurred in branches more sensitive to such events such as commerce, hotels and restaurants, finances, and real estate. In general, the old social structure remained petrified.

Those being the domestic conditions, it was the external factors that came into play. On September 17, 1990, the foreign affairs ministers of the European Economic Community were scheduled to meet in Madrid, and Romania was on top of the agenda. The miners' riot in Bucharest the previous June had been watched with horror on television all over the world, and

Table 1
Distribution of Employment in the Main Sectors of the Economy
(in thousands)

	1989	1990	1991
Total	10,945	10,840	10,786
Industry	4,169	4,005	3,803
Construction	653	705	501
Agriculture	3,012	3,055	3,116
Commerce	493	538	699
Hotels, restaurants	167	186	213
Finance, banks	27	39	44
Real estate and			
other services	330	388	421

Source: Anuarul Statistic al României, 1995.

Romania's image abroad looked appalling. Something had to be done, and quickly, to improve that image, so as to encourage the EEC ministers to include Romania in their aid programs for Eastern Europe. In a newspaper article I suggested that President Iliescu should invite leaders of the opposition to discuss the issue of Romania's international status and that Prime Minister Roman should take steps to accelerate the privatization process. The tone of the article was rather mild and argumentative, and the two did not budge. Then I decided to make a stronger case on television, emphasizing in harsh terms that if President Iliescu and Prime Minister Roman did not act quickly and if, as a result, the EEC ministers maintained the penalty against Romania, *A head would fall!*

The TV interview had the effect of a thunderbolt. The next day, President Iliescu invited the leaders of the opposition to Cotroceni Palace, and Prime Minister Roman made a fulminating speech against those who obstructed privatization. Both saw to it that international press agencies released the news. Shortly afterward, the EEC ministers meeting in Madrid decided to start negotiations with Romania on aid programs. No head had to fall! Finally, in mid-1991 the Roman government adopted a reform program that was applauded even by the opposition. Prices and foreign trade were liberalized; the Law of Industry's Privatization was passed in Parliament as was an agrarian reform giving 80% of the arable land to the peasants. Hence, the process of dislocation of the old social structure was initiated.

THE FIRST SOCIAL EARTHQUAKE

By the end of 1991 the economic situation had gotten worse. Inflation and prices skyrocketed (around 200%), unemployment went up to 1 million, or 11% of the urban workforce. The miners' rampage in September 1991 that toppled Prime Minister Roman expressed, in a most brutal and violent manner, the reaction of industrial workers against the rapid transition to a market economy. They destroyed and looted all private shops in their way—from modest kiosks and individual market stalls of peasants in the town of Petrosani to the new luxury shops with elegant clothes and attractive windows in Bucharest's main boulevard. The furious thrust of miners was reminiscent of the early nineteenth-century English Luddite workers destroying the labor-saving machinery that they perceived as a threat to their jobs.

Everybody was amazed at the complete turnabout in the miners' attitude. In June 1990 they had come in force to Bucharest to save the government and President Iliescu from the threat of the University Plaza anti-communist stronghold. At that time the miners had vented their rage in the streets and in the auditoriums and labs of the university and had devastated the headquarters of the opposition parties and newspapers. This time, in the fall of 1991, the coal miners of the Jiu Valley staged their assault on the nation's capital with a diametrically opposite aim: to topple Roman's government. Why such a radical reversal?

We are reminded that, in the meantime, starting in September 1990, Roman had switched to a shock-therapy strategy. Prices were liberalized in three stages, rising three or four times; particularly painful for wage-earners was the decision to cut from the budget the subsidies for food items that had compensated workers for their depressed wages. With the adoption of the privatization law, the specter of massive unemployment was turning the workers into an angry and unruly crowd. Moreover, they saw that the real beneficiaries of the revolution were the new businessmen and entrepreneurs, who were making a fast buck while they, the workers, had become the underdogs of society. That was the social background of the miners' violent protest. It was not accidental that the reaction came from the social category most threatened by the harsh laws of the market and modernization. This was also true of Madam Thatcher's coal miners in Sheffield, and President Yeltsin's miners in Donbass.

THE DISLOCATION PROCESS

While the 1990 elections reflected the old social structure, in the 1992 elections, as a result of changes in economic life, the first shake-up of this structure could be observed. The liberalization of prices and foreign trade; the privatization of trade, light industry, and services; as well as the blow dealt to collective farms by the Land Act—all strongly rattled the old system of social relations and opened up a process of deep-reaching transformation in Romanian society.

Industrial workers, proclaimed by the communists as the leading class, recorded a significant numerical decline. As can be seen in Table 2, the most dramatic fall was in manufacturing, as the miners' rampages had succeeded in maintaining the number of those employed in the coal industry.

Table 2
Workers Occupied in Various Industries (in thousands)

	1990	1991	1995
Total industries	4005	3803	2601.1
Extractions	259	277	243
Manufacturing	3613	3372	2191.7
Energy, electric,			
gas & water	133	154	166.5
Constructions	706	501	506

Source: Anuarul Statistic al României, 1995.

What made the transition so effervescent in Eastern Europe was the sudden change in the social status of workers. No political leader in the East today will dare to admit publicly that market reform, coupled with assimilation of new technologies, actually is going against the interests of what used to be called the dominant working class. The stark and bitter truth is that workers are the great losers of the revolution. They are requested to work harder and better—which they resent, not being accustomed to that; they are faced with the specter of unemployment—something they had never experienced and which scares and irritates them. Gone are job security and the special opportunities for education and political careers they had enjoyed in the past. No more workers in the government or in parliament. Small wonder that the sense of becoming the underdog of society makes workers strike not only for economic grievances, but also for political reasons. Their ideological confusion is total, which facilitates their manipulation by politicians.

Beginning in 1993, a marked process of differentiation has taken place within the social classes as a result of privatization and change of ownership. The working class no longer functions as a large and compact sociological unit. As shown in

Table 3, the most dynamic mutation has taken place in man-ufacturing: In March 1995, out of 2,498,055 workers, 333,584 were employed in private enterprises, and 83,639 in mixed firms, which means that 17% had left the state sector. In con-struction, there was a massive migration from the state sec-tor to private, mixed, and cooperatist enterprises—79%. As might be expected, the private sector had attracted a large percentage of employees in commerce, hotels, and restau-rants. But the most spectacular social transition had oc-curred in agriculture, as a result of the agrarian reform. In March 1995, only 8% of the active rural population re-mained in the state sector. More than 5 million had become land owners (about 40% from urban areas). As 9 million hectares were now divided into 20 million small plots that could hardly make use of tractors and modern farming methods, many joined large cooperatist associations (about 3,800) or commercial capitalist farms based on shares (about 518); their number has been growing rapidly. It is in-teresting to note that, as compared with 1989, more than a half million people have moved from cities to the country-side as land owners.

In general, at the end of 1995, the private sector repre-sented:

35% of the GNP

14% of the industry

70.1% of the arable land

70.5% of the commerce

43.6% of the services

40.5% of the export

44.8% of the import.

The more or less egalitarian society of communism was now polarized in Romania: At one pole over a million jobless peo-ple and 3 to 4 million living under the poverty line; at the

Table 3
Population Occupied According to Ownership (March 1995)

Economic activities	Total active population	Public	Private	Mixed	Cooperatist	Other
Total	11,152,273	5,601,070	5,213,695	175,465	132,560	29,482
Agriculture	4,426,258	351,966	4,038,799	32,314	3,179	
Industry—extraction	281,542	271,178	6,815	3,549		
Industry—manufacturing	2,498,055	2,010,076	333,584	83,639	70,755	
Energy, gas, water	204,351	201,976		2,374		
Construction	468,137	300,655	141,162	19,911	5,888	
Commerce	716,959	222,847	453,880	13,820	25,480	
Hotels & restaurants	138,199	58,103	65,217	4,076	3,874	6,929
Transportation	437,826	370,403	57,365	9,665		
Post, telecommunications	118,810	114,422	4,388			
Finance, banks	87,084	72,863	9,775	2,247	2,200	
Real estate	153,411	123,862	24,858		3,835	
Public administration, defense	562,770	560,243				
Education	436,313	429,872	6,441			
Health	345,238	332,417	10,515			
Other activities	205,948	113,806	56,339		15,238	18,957

Source: Anuarul Statistic al României, 1996.

other pole, the economy has spawned millionaires and even billionaires in only five years.

In Poland, the political editor of *Gazeta Wyborcza* described the division of Polish society thusly: Among those favored by the market reform—the political elite, entrepreneurs, businessmen, and the intelligentsia; among those negatively affected—workers in obsolete industries, white-collar workers whose salaries cannot keep pace with inflation, and peasants who cannot compete with food items imported from Western Europe. Fourteen percent are unemployed, and one of three families live under the poverty line.

In a 1994 article on polarization, I concluded that this phenomenon will last until a middle class takes center stage in our society. Indeed, in developed societies it is the middle class that is the stabilizing factor. Therefore, let us focus on the formation of the middle class in Eastern European countries.

INTRODUCTION TO THE MIDDLE CLASS

The middle class is responsible for the invalidation of Karl Marx's nineteenth-century prognosis that future society will be divided between capitalists and workers. Therefore, the notion of a middle class in communist countries was taboo. Most studies on the subject have been made in the United States, the country that gave birth to the largest middle class in the history of capitalism. Max Lerner emphasizes that earlier in American history the middle class comprised the independent farmers, the small businessmen and shopkeepers, the professions, and the middlemen. Later, white-collar groups joined that class, and, after World War II, even highly paid workers in the steel and automobile industries qualified as middle class. "They form a loose collection of occupational strata," writes Lerner. He continues: "they are caught in a kind of Purgatory between the Hell of the poor and weak, and the Heaven of the rich and powerful."[1] Eventually, he provides a general definition: "The middle classes do not hold the power of government or rule the economy; they do rule the culture, set the tone of consumption, serve as the crucial audience for the Big Media. They are in a sense the pivot class of America."[2]

In Western Europe also after World War II, a large contingent of the industrial workers jumped into the middle class, getting access to such items (automobiles, houses, vacations abroad, and so forth) that had been considered to be prerogatives of the bourgeoisie. In the Golden Age of capitalism, which Eric Hobsbawm situates between 1950 and 1970, the number of American tourists traveling abroad grew from 300,000 to 7 million annually. The European figures were even more spectacular. Spain, which had virtually no mass tourism until the later 1950s, welcomed over 54 million foreigners per year—a number only slightly surpassed by Italy's 55 million. What had once been luxury became the expected standard of comfort for many people.[3] Romanians on the Black Sea were surprised to meet foreigners who told them they were simple workers at home. The chairman of a Romanian trade union returning from a Labor Congress in England told his friends in astonishment: "Do you realize, the comrades up there own a home and a car!" Small wonder that the British Labour Party was considered *middle-class socialism*!

Middle classes are not the same everywhere. Unlike the American middle class, which has a flexible capacity to adjust itself to various contingencies, the middle class in Germany tends to be rigid and amorphous. Max Weber saw it caught in an "iron cage" between workers and capitalists; as a result, when economic disaster gripped Germany, the middle classes were wiped out by inflation and thrown into the arms of the Nazis by political hysteria. In France, a special place in the configuration of the middle class is held by *les cadres*, the three million engineers, managers, specialists, and those in the liberal professions, whose life-style has left its mark on French social life.

C. Wright Mills, whose book on the middle class has become a classic, described them in very expressive terms: "The white-collar people slipped quietly into modern society. Whatever history they have had is a history without events; whatever common interests they have do not lead to unity; whatever future they have will not be of their own making. If they aspire at all, it is to a middle course, at a time when no middle course is available, and hence to an illusory course, in an imaginary society. Internally, they are split, fragmented; externally, they are dependent on larger forces."[4]

THE MIDDLE CLASS: KEY FACTOR IN MARKET REFORM

The evaluation of progress in post-communist societies is usually made in terms of political and economic achievements. Seldom are changes in the social sphere taken into account, although these affect society much more profoundly and are more indicative in regard to both present stability and the future of our nations. Examining the social stratification of these societies, we will find at the top of the common phenomenon of the rapid enrichment of capitalists, involving in most cases enterprising members of the communist *nomenklatura*. However, as we go down to the bottom and the middle of society, an obvious discrepancy appears between the Central European nations and Russia. The name of that discrepancy is *the middle class*.

To better understand the genesis and dynamics of the middle class in Eastern Europe, we must go back to the pre-communist era. In Central Europe, the motive force of social development was capitalist-industrial growth, while in Russia, rigid feudal structures with millions of illiterate peasants were dominant. Apparently, in the Russia of modern times there has always been one class lagging behind the historical

process. In October 1917, when the task was the socialist revolution, the supposed social agent of change, the *proletariat*,
was missing. Today, when the task is the building of a market
economy, it is the *middle class* that is missing. American historian Richard Pipes makes a perceptive point: "Russia's inabil-
ity to produce a large and vigorous bourgeoisie is usually
seen as a major cause of its deviation from the political patterns of Western Europe and of the failure of liberal ideas to
significantly influence its political institutions and practices."
Russian historian Yuri Afanasiev also emphasizes that in Russia today the lack of a social base for democratic reformists is
leading to an oligarchic system.

Not so in Central Europe. In Czechoslovakia, where the inter-war regime of President Massarick was on a par with Western Europe in terms of capitalist-industrial development and
democracy, even during the four decades of communism a
powerful social stratum survived, enjoying a standard of living characteristic of a middle class (house ownership, automobile, significant cultural expenditures, holiday abroad,
and the like). For obvious ideological reasons, official statistics never mentioned that category, but Western sociologists
discovered that, in the 1970s and 1980s, families with high incomes and a middle-class life-style in Czechoslovakia represented about 30% of the active population; in Hungary, the
figure was 20% to 25%; in Poland, 15%. In retrospect, we
now realize that the "Prague Spring" and the reformist drive
that swept Hungary and Poland actually reflected petit-bour-
geois trends toward liberalization and market rather than
typical working-class grievances.

In 1982, while visiting Hungary on a research project, I discovered that an extensive system of auxiliary activities had
taken shape in industry and services, all private, so that only
25% of consumer services were performed by the state enterprises. Almost all the food stores in Budapest were private. High
incomes were also achieved in agriculture: about 4 million people were tending private plots of up to 6,000 square meters.

It all began with the historic party resolution of May 7, 1966, ten years after the social earthquake that shook Hungary: "The development of an active role for the market requires the cumbersome and bureaucratic state system of the centralized allocation of materials and products to give place to commercial relations, i.e., producers should be able to decide within their range of activities what and how much they produce and offer for sale, as well as from whom they purchase the necessary inputs." The wording sounded revolutionary, but the implementation was gradual and prudent.

To do away with the old anachronistic system, the Kadar government began by relaxing its control over individual enterprises; local managers were given a greater say in investment, production, and price decisions, while the state retained overall control through credit, price, wage, and foreign trade "regulators." The success of the economic reform was particularly evident in agriculture. An ingenious relationship was created between the large socialist cooperatives and the private plots of farmers, essentially based on material incentive.

The average size of the household plot in Hungary was small, but cultivated intensively. Istran Szendrei, in his late fifties, was a member of the nearby Bocskai Cooperative. He and his wife earned one-third of their income from raising 75 to 85 pigs per year and cultivating poppies. Imre Vince belonged to the younger generation and was more aggressive. He raised independently 500 to 600 pigs per year in a backyard of about 4,000 square metres, buying fodder from the cooperative. He and his family could afford two compact cars and could spend the holiday driving to Italy. Surely, all those farmers were better prepared for the market economy than were the Soviet *kolkhozniki*.

The formation of the middle class in Hungary has been thoroughly studied by the Hungarian sociologist Rudolf Andorka. He noted that, between 1980 and 1990, an approach toward the capitalist societies could be observed in terms of the proportion of self-employed artisans and merchants, which increased strongly, and to that of peasants, which began to increase. Measured by the average per capita household income, managers and professionals were on top of the hierarchy, clericals and skilled workers were the middle categories, and non-skilled workers and peasants were at the bottom. After the 1989 revolution, income inequalities among those strata began to grow. While managers and self-employed entrepreneurs, artisans, and merchants were able to increase their personal income much more than the inflation rate (about 74%, from 1989 to 1991), those with fixed wages suffered a loss of real income.[5] Whereas in the 1980s about a million persons (19% of the population) had an income lower than the subsistence minimum, by 1992–1993 this number had increased to 20%–25%.

I. Szeleny speaks of two alternatives with regard to the development of the middle class: either a strong and large bourgeoisie develops from the strata that were earlier active in the second economy (around 21% of the national income) and became small private entrepreneurs after the revolution, or a "comprador" bourgeoisie serving the big—partly multi-national—enterprises emerges. Government policy favoring either domestic or foreign capital will be crucial in deciding which way the bourgeoisie will develop. Thus, an intensive discussion took place in Hungary on the *embourgeoisement* of Hungarian society. Szeleny thinks that if the term refers to people with moderately high incomes, enjoying financial security and a high level of education and culture, then *embourgeoisement* is almost synonymous with the growth of the middle class.[6]

Romania was left behind the Central European countries in this respect. *Breviarul Statistic* reveals that in the inter-war period the urban petit-bourgeoisie was made up of 128,000 owners, 327,000 store managers, 25,100 liberal professionals, and 19,500 family members: in total, 3%–5% of the active population. Under communism, a study published by the Center for Sociological Research in 1988 showed that a "higher status" in society (in terms of housing comfort, cultural consumption, cars, and the like) was enjoyed by 5% of the active population. Such a low percentage was caused by Ceausescu's statist policy, which stifled any private economic activity. Even private peasants and owners of household plots were harassed by the militia whenever they tried to sell their produce on the market.

In the Soviet Union, besides the party and state dignitaries enjoying high salaries, only artists, musicians, and scientists as well as managers who worked in the military-industrial complex, had a higher income. They represented no more than 1% of the active population. Sociologist Mikhail Tchernich considers that this very thin stratum taking shape after Gorbachev's opening of *perestroika* in 1985 had a monthly income of between $250 and $2,000 per person and usually owned an apartment, an automobile, a TV set, an imported last-generation refrigerator, a magnetoscope, and a small dacha outside town.

As shown in Table 4 there is an almost mathematical relationship between the percentage of a potential middle class before 1989 and the progress of the market reform as of 1995. The Czech Republic, with a 30% potential middle class, had become the front-runner, with more than $4,000 per capita in Gross Domestic Product (GDP) and an average monthly wage of $300. Hungary and Poland followed closely. Romania, with only a 5% potential middle class, was trailing the group in 1995, with $1,380 per capita in GDP and an average monthly wage of about $100—three times poorer than the Central European nations. Certainly, the Czech Republic and Hungary had enjoyed a massive influx of foreign investment, but it was the more appropriate social structure that led to a higher GDP and average monthly wage. Russia, despite its enormous natural riches, has been seriously hampered in economic development by its lack of a middle class. To repeat: *the middle class is the key to success in market reform.*

Table 4
Transition in Post-Communist Societies

| | | | 1995 | | |
Countries	Potential middle class before 1989 (%)	Per capita GDP ($)	Average monthly wage ($)	Foreign investment per capita ($)	GDP growth (%)
Czech Republic	30	4,338	303.1	533.9	4
Slovakia	25	2,926	253.0	132.0	6.4
Hungary	20–25	3,882	328.0	970.9	4.0
Poland	15	3,167	307.0	155.4	6.5
Romania	5	1,380	110.0	79.3	3.8
Bulgaria	5	1,176	118.0	94.1	2.8
Albania	1	332	50.0	—	6.0
Russia	1	2,393	126.3	—	–2.0

Source: Financial Times and Business Central Europe.

RUSSIA—NO MIDDLE CLASS

I emphasized earlier the discrepancy between the social evolution in Central Europe and Russia. The issue is sufficiently important to require a deeper examination. To begin with, whereas in Central Europe the capitalists could not be wiped out during four decades of communist rule, in Russia the few capitalists existing in 1917 were completely crushed, even physically exterminated, in seventy years of communism. Therefore, the new social structure of capitalism in Russia had to start from scratch. It was much easier for the big guys to hit the jackpot and become millionaires in control of major Russian enterprises and banks. The middle class, however, is a matter of numbers. We are dealing here with a class whose impact on society is effective only when its membership is sufficiently large to represent a high proportion of the population.

Without a large middle class the market economy cannot take shape and function; therefore, its re-emergence in Russia was a must. The new middle-class in Russia originated first in the economic state apparatus. This process began in 1985 with Gorbachev's *perestroika*. The investigations of Russian sociologists reveal that the first businessmen were bureaucrats who kept their jobs. Tatiana Zaslavskaya, the well-known sociologist, in 1993 undertook a study of a representative sample of 24,354 people engaged in economic activities. Seven percent owned their own businesses but remained on the state payroll at the same time. For those, Zaslavskaya invented the term "part-time businessmen"—persons who did not drop out of the state economy, did not even identify themselves with their new social status. She emphasizes that quite a few managers of big commercial companies maintained their positions in the state sector.

Economist V. V. Radaev, who examined managers of companies with stockholders, found out that more than three quarters of them were at the same time co-owners, while 6%

held sufficient shares to control the company. He makes a distinction between "classical managers," who worked both in state and private spheres (467), and co-owner managers, who worked only in the private sphere (173).

The conclusion is that in the transition period, a Russian stratum of entrepreneurs (Zaslavskaya avoids calling them capitalists) has acquired a relatively high social position. The income of entrepreneurs-owners is twice as great as that of simple businessmen and five times greater than that of wage earners. Russian sociologists complain that respondents are reluctant to reveal their real income and that about 30% of revenues are cashed in by racketeers for guaranteeing protection to businessmen. They all indicate that their samples are limited: the big capitalists are not included.

There is a striking difference between the courage of big tycoons who venture into the spectacular acquisitions of state goods and capital and the timidity of owners of small workshops, commercial stores, and services. The former think that power is behind them, whereas the latter must fight bureaucracy and the mentality of the population, which is hostile to businessmen. The anachronistic social structure makes the transition of Russian society to capitalism a tough exercise.

And yet, slowly but surely, the social inequalities characteristic of capitalism are making their way in that "classless society." A Russian social inquiry in 1995 noted that in 1991, that is, shortly before the liberalization of consumer prices, the ratio of the average income per household in the lowest income category to the 10% with the highest income was 1:4.1. A year later, in November 1992, this ratio between the incomes of the poorest and the richest 10% had widened to 1:8.8, and, in May 1993, the highest-income 10% received an average of 10.5 points more than the 10% with the lowest income in St. Petersburg. In other words, the gap between the rich and the poor in a major urban center of Russia became more than twice as wide in only two years.

One of the peculiarities in Russia's transition period has been the ability of a household to invest its resources in additional sectors of economic activity in order to maximize its well-being. For example, in addition to work and consumption in the official economy, where, as a popular saying has it, "We pretend to work and they pretend to pay us," many Russians direct their efforts to the *second economy* or *shadow economy*. Here, though payments are in money, the exchange of goods and services is "unofficial" in the sense that no official records on the transactions are being kept; therefore, such activities are not subject to taxation. Second economy jobs may have the character of part-time employment; an employee in a state-owned enterprise may repair cars or TV sets, give piano lessons, drive a taxi without a license, or sell home-sewn clothing. According to cautious estimates, the size of the shadow economy in Russia represents approximately 20% of the GNP, and more daring appraisals go as far as 50% of the GNP.

A practice associated with the distribution of scarce goods (Janos Kornai called it the "Economy of Shortage") has been omnipresent in Russia from the time of the tsars: *bribes*. In the post-communist period, which has been marked by political confusion and the absence of adequate legislation, the practice of bribery has assumed magnificent proportions. To begin with, the salaries in the budgetary organizations are so low that bribe-taking may be practically a necessity for the survival of a public servant. As the state retains enormous power in economic life, its functionaries enjoy the power to make decisions so that the size of bribes ranges from the giant payoffs given to decision makers by the new entrepreneurs or foreign investors wishing to receive an official permit for their business to the bottle of vodka for a driver's license. We are reminded of a remark made by the famous nineteenth-century novelist M. E. Saltykov-Shchedrin: "In Russia money is better invested in bribes than in bank deposits!"

To sum up: In Russia, the formation of a middle class originates both in the economic state apparatus and in a series of private activities initiated by the most enterprising citizens who know the ropes. At the time of this social inquiry (1995) the share of the active population represented by people with a middle-class position in Russian society was no more than 1%, but it is growing fast. It is the lack of this factor of stability in modern society that makes this author reluctant to predict the future development of Russia.

IN ROMANIA: A WILD MIDDLE CLASS

The answer to the question of how the middle class was born in Romania is: *with forceps*. The formation of a middle class was a must after 1989. The market economy could not take shape and function with workers and peasants alone; it requires merchants and entrepreneurs, shopkeepers and salesmen, commercial agents and bankers, bookkeepers and managers, exporters and importers. Far from the slow and gradual process that took decades in the West, in Eastern Europe a fast and accelerated tempo was imperative. That is why access to the middle class is not always kosher. Very often people resort to fraud and deception, falsehood and bribery. Angry and justiciary headlines appear on the front pages of newspapers every day denouncing ingenious fraudulent schemes and scandalous swindles that are making "big holes" in the state budget and contraband acts involving tons of cigarettes, coffee, or whiskey; but these may be regarded as nothing but daring feats of those who face dangers and take risks in order to forge the new middle class of Romania.

In this respect we Romanians are not at all innovators. The Caritas pyramid-like fraud, as well as the Bragonads or Bahaians of Bucharest, have predecessors in the most respectable capitals of the West. The telespectators who watch in great admiration the serial dedicated to the glamorous living of the Kennedy family would be terribly disappointed to find out that the founder of the family, Joe Kennedy, made his fortune as a bootlegger during Prohibition. Gradually, the new status-seekers acquire a culture and life-style typical to the middle class, thus becoming respectable citizens of the country.

Applying the methodology of establishing the social hierarchy on the basis of *income* in underdeveloped Romania, where $100 is the average monthly wage, we estimate the threshold of the middle class at a net monthly income of 2 million lei (about $300 at the 1997 rate), and its ceiling at 10 million lei (about $1,500). Who are the lucky ones who qualify?

1. *Persons with fixed incomes, in the state sector:*
   (a) Top dignitaries (president, prime minister, and members of the cabinet, senators, deputies, generals, high magistrates, and the like);
   (b) Managers of autonomous public enterprises with monthly salaries higher than 2 million lei;
2. *Owners, shareholders, executives, bank managers in the private sector,* including directors of foreign companies and subsidiary banks with salaries paid in dollars. As no law has yet been adopted that would establish a tax on personal income, no such situation is available in the private sector;
3. *Members of boards of directors* in state institutions administering public property;
4. *"Parallel" or underground economy.*

In 1994, Virgil Magureanu, director of the Romanian Information Service, estimated that illegal business and "money laundering" represented 38% of the Gross National Product. As the press began to reveal the magnitude of such operations involving tens and hundreds of billions, the above-mentioned percentage no longer looked exaggerated. The names of such "operators" as Zaher Iskandarani, the "prince of Banat," Vasile Gheorhe, alias Gigi Kent, and such mafiosi as Fane Spoitoru and Raducanu became famous. Their methods were as ingenious as they were profitable. Full train wagons with goods, huge trucks with millions of boxes of cigarettes, and tons of coffee and whiskey passed through custom check-points as through open doors. One such individual, Costal Moldovan, smuggled seventeen automobiles without paying custom duties. Like mushrooms after the rain, thousands of "fly-by-night" companies suddenly appeared without having an office site. It is reasonable to assume that those who undertake such risks would not be satisfied with less than 2 million lei a month, thus qualifying with flying colors for the middle class. Their number is of the order of thousands.

In estimating the size of the middle class, one must take into account the fact that there are about 400,000 subscribers to mutual funds (such as SAFI, CIRO, ARDAF) whose average investments exceed 2 million lei. More than a million individuals have opened bank accounts; some banks have established a minimum of 5 million lei, or $1,000. Hence, a substantial middle class has already taken shape in Romania, seeking to take center stage in society. Their members represent the main consumption force in durable goods, automobiles, and house construction. In only six months of 1995 they bought 25,000 cars from the Korean company Daewoo at a special price, $20,000. Members of the middle class are the chief promoters of Romanian tourism—domestic and abroad—every evening they patronize the numerous luxury restaurants where a dinner costs the minimum monthly wage. All in all, the middle class in Romania has been growing fast, by the end of 1996 approaching 10% of the active population.

MILLIONAIRES IN FIVE YEARS!
HOW DID THEY DO IT?

Because the accumulation of private capital was forbidden legally and condemned morally in communist society, after 1989 *the capitalist class took shape at the expense of the state,* grabbing state property and taking hold, through privatization, of state machine tools and production. Of course, in the forefront of this large-scale robbery were the former party and state bureaucrats holding strategic positions that allowed them to operate quickly and with great efficiency. A study on one hundred top Russian businessmen undertaken by the Institute of Applied Politics in Moscow found that 60% belong to the former *nomenklatura*. A Polish economist who examined the evolution of several hundreds of former party bureaucrats in the period 1988–1993 discovered that more than half of those became managers in the private sector; and in Hungary the percentage was even higher.

Again, Russia had led the way. Russia, with its enormous riches and natural resources, naturally qualified in the vanguard of this historical plunder, its entrepreneurs showing an unexpected ingenuity after seventy years of bolshevism. Serghey Yegorov, former president of the USSR Statebank and head of the Financial Section of the C.C. of C.P.S.U., has become the president of Commerce Banking Association, a tycoon worth hundreds of millions of dollars; Nikolai Rijkov, former prime minister at the time of Gorbachev, is president of Tveruniversal Bank, while Piotr Aven, former minister of commerce, is president of Alpha Bank. Ranking at the top, Prime Minister Viktor Cernomyrdin was director of the gigantic gas company Gazprom, which was secretly privatized through a method that allowed the former boss to take the lion's share. It is interesting to note that while the oil industry was fractured into a dozen holding companies, Gazprom managed to inherit the state natural gas monopoly intact, with assets bigger than those of General Motors. In 1995, Cernomyrdin created for the elections a party called *Nash Dom* (Our House); the Russians used to call it *Nash Dom Gazprom*.

Since the post-Soviet millionaires started making a fortune in the Gorbachev years of "thaw," they now enjoy *The Commercial Club*, an elegant building at No. 2 Bolshaya Kommunisticheskaya Ulitsa, with three luxury restaurants, a casino, and a series of meeting rooms—all arranged like an exclusive English club. An American journalist described a visit to this club the day the manager presented a glossy new almanac of entrepreneurs entitled *The Rebirth of the Russian Business Elite.* Dozens of BMWs, Mercedes, Jeep Cherokees, and Lincoln Town Cars were lined up at the curb. Well-dressed men and sable-swathed women headed for the entrance. Their bodyguards, with pistols and machine guns bulging from their jackets, stayed close by. Ten businessmen were listed in the almanac as *super-elite.* I shall mention some of them with their Kremlin connections.

Vladimir Potanin, chairman of Uneximbank (Export Import) was an intimate friend of Lieutenant General Alexander Korshakov, a former KGB high officer, who was Kremlin security chief in 1993–1995 and Boris Yeltsin's close associate and tennis and drinking partner. Uneximbank was already a powerhouse when it dreamed up a "loans for shares" scheme, whereby the government was offered quick cash to plug budgetary holes in return for imprecisely defined enterprises. Acting both as auctioneer and bidder, Uneximbank snatched up controlling stakes in the Arctic mining colossus Norilsk Nickel, the world's biggest nickel producer, and the gigantic Sidanco, for the combined price of $300 million—a hundred times lower than its real value. A newspaperman revealed that at the auction, the $179 million offered by the bank surpassed by only $100,000 the starting minimal offer set by the same Uneximbank, which was appointed by the government to conduct the auction.

Using the same method, Uneximbank, with its Interros financial-industrial holding, brought fifteen more heavyweights from the metal and petrochemical industries into the Uneximbank orbit. Everything was carried out in perfect order under the handy cover of privatization. Anatoli Chubais, as he was sacked from the post of first deputy prime minister, disclosed to the press that special customs privileges awarded in secret by Yeltsin to his cronies were costing the government more than $800 million each year in lost revenue.

Mikhail Khodorovsky, president of the famous bank Menatep, came right from the Communist Youth League leadership and very quickly established his reputation as the brassy
bad-boy genius of post-Soviet finance. Menatep was the first
"brat pack" bank to crack the charmed circle of authorized
agents for state investment programs. Always in close contact
with the Kremlin, Menatep in 1995 arranged a mysterious
government purchase of 15% of the bank's shares. Very soon,
Menatep grabbed the Yukos oil empire in the "loans-for-
shares" melee—a transaction that got the management's bless-
ing—for cash.

Recently, Moscow newspapers published a taped conversa-
tion of an influential man named Boris Fydorov in which he
described the way big business was reaching into Yeltsin's inner circle. Fydorov, age 36, was head of the National Sports
Fund, an organization that was granted special status by
Yeltsin in December 1993, thereby benefiting from huge tax
breaks on the importation of alcohol and cigarettes. The subsidy had cost the government $200 million a month, up to a
total of $6 billion in tax revenue. Once that special status was
withdrawn in 1995, Boris Fydorov decided to talk, printing a
chilling picture of high-level corruption involving Sports
Minister Shamil Tarpischev, Lt. Gen. Alexander Korzhakov,
and Mikhail Barsukov, all three intimate friends and tennis
and drinking partners of Yeltsin's. *Novaya Ezhednevnaya*, a
Moscow daily paper, described the group as President Yeltsin's inner circle, which had made the tough decisions of the
Kremlin, including Chechenia, until the 1996 presidential
elections.

Another clan of big business is centered around Yuri M.
Luzhkov, the mayor of Moscow. His favorite tycoon is Vladimir
Gusinski, the leading entrepreneur in Russia according to
polls. In 1994, Gusinski was worth as much as $50 million.
That does not make him the richest man in Russia, but as
owner of the leading liberal newspaper *Segodnya* (Today), of
the radio station *Ekho Moskvy*, and of the main independent

television channel, he is certainly the most influential one. A pioneer in commercial banking and real estate, head of a vast holding company called MOST, and a media mogul, Gusinski flies in his personal jet, his cars are bullet-proof, and he lives in a dacha compound outside Moscow equipped with electronic fences. As an international operator, he owns apartments in London and Paris and vacations in Spain and Portugal; his son is a student in a Swiss boarding school. Gusinski is deeply embroiled in Kremlin politics, and, as such, one of his leading advisers is Fillip Bobkov, a former deputy chairman of the KGB.

How did Gusinski make his fortune? During the early *perestroika days*, Gusinski cultivated friends in the Ministry of Foreign Economic Relations, making connections that made it easier for him to travel abroad and meet foreign businessmen. Working with a Washington-based law firm, he began a joint venture, a sort of consulting firm that advised foreign clients on potential markets in the Soviet Union. With the dollars he earned and with the support of his good friend, Mayor Luzhkov, Gusinski bought up dozens of dachas and properties around Moscow from ruined *nomenklaturists*, refurbished them, and then sold them to the *nouveaux riches* for prices many times their cost. That was how he founded the MOST bank and set up its headquarters right in Mayor Luzhkov's City Hall.

Piotr Aven, a former minister of Foreign Trade and now the president of Alpha Bank, told the *Moscow News:* "Often it is enough to have active support in the government, the Parliament, local power structures and law-enforcement agencies. One fine day, your insignificant bank is authorized to conduct operations with budgetary funds, for instance. Or quotas for the export of oil, timber, and gas are generously allotted to your company, which is in no way connected with production. In other words, you are appointed a millionaire."[7]

A typical tycoon who knows the right mix between business and politics is Oleg Boyko. As a college student in the early *perestroika* days, he realized the importance of computers and, with little money, began to import secondhand computers and software; he quickly built a $1.5-billion empire of banks, retail stores, and real estate, always staying in favor with the Kremlin. Initially, Boyko supported Vice Premier Yegor Gaidar, but when his sponsor resigned in protest against the Chechen war, Boyko switched to Premier Cernomyrdin and his Nash Dom. The clan of pro-Yeltsin magnates is known as the "Big Eight," a consortium of major banks and companies, including Menatep, Stolichny, and Boyko's Imperial Bank. Journalists refer to the group as "The Octopus," because its tentacles seem entangled in every major economic venture. A breathtakingly bold proposal was characteristic of the consortium's capital-power symbiosis: in 1995 it offered to loan $2 billion to the debt-ridden government, in exchange for the government's stake in thousands of state enterprises.

David Remnick painted a perfect portrait of the new Russian capitalist class: "Evidence of the new class is no longer confined to a few streets or hotels, as it was a couple of years ago. It is everywhere, in the form of billboards and television ads; the limos and the Jeeps; the new luxury stores and restaurants sprouting all over town; the pull-out business section of *Izvestia*; the mini-mansions called *kottedzhy*, on the edge of towns, the foreigners roaming the hotel lobbies and ministry hallways, as if looking for the next nugget from the Klondike. You see the new Russian rich in first-class lounges in airports from Vienna to Los Angeles. They fly to New York and London on business. They go on shopping runs to Paris and low-duty havens in the United Arab Emirates."[8]

In March 1993, Len Karpinski, a leading liberal thinker, wrote in the *Moscow News:* "If the bureaucrat continues to be pivotal to the system, we may well find ourselves living under *nomenklatura capitalism*, whose despotism will not be inferior to the planned socialist system." Yuri Afanasiev, historian and former leader of the Democratic Russia movement, also feels that from the ruins of totalitarian communism has risen an oligarchic system in which politics is played out according to the interest of bureaucrats, entrepreneurs, and mafiosi. These people have proven to be genuine prophets. It turned out that the biggest organized crime leaders had an even keener sense of the post-Soviet future than did the politicians. As revealed in the Russian press, already in mid-December 1991, thirty of the top mobsters held a secret meeting at a dacha outside Moscow. They foresaw that the collapse of the communist system would lead to an economic free-for-all situation and decided to take advantage of these unprecedented opportunities.

The cozy partnership of big business and the Kremlin was once more demonstrated in November 1996 as the media mogul and rakish business tycoon Boris Berezovski was appointed deputy chief of the National Security Council. Berezovsky, chairman of Logovaz, Russia's largest car dealership, in 1994 had persuaded the government to sell off 49% of the state-owned network, ORT, to a consortium of Kremlin-favored companies, thus becoming the real boss of the country's biggest network. Berezovsky was one of the select number of business executives who bankrolled Yeltsin's re-election campaign; accordingly, his appointment to such an important position in the state administration was the right choice after General Lebed's tempestuous ouster.

NOMENKLATURISTS EVERYWHERE

The perpetuation of the old *nomenklaturists* in leading positions, political and economic, characterizes the transition period in all Eastern European countries. The party bureaucrats have passed with unexpected easiness from the central or local party headquarters onto the boards of big companies or banks. The remark of a former American diplomat in Budapest turned director of a New York investment bank is very significant: "Whenever I have a meeting at a big Hungarian company, I face over the table somebody I had to deal with at the time when Hungary was communist." As we shall see, Romanian *nomenklaturists* have proven no less aggressive than their Russian, Hungarian, or Polish counterparts. Apparently, the conquest of big business positions in Poland followed closely the Russian model. Therefore, a social case study of Poland is in order.

The Polish publication *Wprost* made a thorough inquiry of more than two hundred managers of the most important Polish companies. The intention was to find out what kind of people were executives and board members of major companies and which names were listed most often. The inquiry revealed entrepreneurs involved in strategic arrangements, businessmen closely connected with political leaders in power, sometimes acting as their advisers and regular companions in state visits abroad. In most cases, they were coming from the communist *nomenklatura,* having rapidly adapted to the market economy. Such businessmen now enjoy tremendous wealth, participate in many enterprises, and exercise great influence in state affairs. In exchange for their services as advisers and consultants, they expect from the government the most important commodity: inside information. And, as we shall see, they have not been disappointed. The reader will find in the Polish case study many similarities with the advent of the Romanian millionaires whom we shall deal with in the next section. Special attention should be paid to those involved in foreign trade.

In Poland, the big contracts regarding state orders and public works swallow one-fifth of the national budget. It has become a general practice to organize the auctions for such contracts according to the following procedure: The companies are invited on such short notice that they have very little time to prepare an offer; therefore, only the firm that knew in advance the nature and conditions of the business is in a position to present a well-documented offer. Such a procedure was used in the case of Intercontinental Hotel in Bucharest: The major international company Marriot lost the building, although it offered a higher price, because the Romanian bidder came in with a complete offer.

In Poland, on top of the list are the former managers of state enterprises dealing with foreign trade, including Elektrim, Budimex, Impexmetal, Kolmex, Kopex, Hortex, CIECH, and Stalexport. All of these enterprises have been privatized through the MEBO method (whereby managers or workers buy the enterprise, which will be described in detail with respect to Romania in the following section), the managers keeping their positions, of course. Most of these managers can be found in the delegations that accompany President Alexander Kwasniewski and Prime Minister W. Lodzimierz Kimosewicz in state visits abroad.

The man to be found most often in the presidential airplane is Andrzej Skowronski, general director of Elektrim, the largest holding company in Poland. Elektrim controls more than one hundred enterprises in electricity, telecommunications, and the agro-food business. In 1994 its net profit was 520 billion zlotys. Elektrim has invested in all enterprises with a future: highway construction (66.57% of Autostrada Wielkopolska), development of cellular telephones (32.5% of Polska Telefonia Cyfrowa SRL), and mass media (TV and newspapers). Skowronski was a member of the Presidential Council of Businessmen and is a board member of the cable factory Bydgoszcz, of Polifarb, Warta, and other major companies. He has participated in the most important state visits of the president and of the prime minister.

Another prominent figure among Polish businessmen is Grzegorz Tuderek, general director and president of Budimex SA (the former Foreign Trade Construction Enterprise), now the largest construction company in Poland. Beginning in 1990, Budimex bought, for 5.5 billion zlotys, the telegraph company and other enterprises. Initially, Tuderek supported President Walesa, but in 1995 he lent his support to President Kwasniewski. Tuderek accompanied the president to the Davos World Economic Forum and to Moscow.

The list of top businessmen would be incomplete without the name of Edward Wojtulewicz, president of Impexmetal SA, which has swallowed up all Polish foundries, becoming the most important holding company in the metal industry. Wojtulewicz is a member of the boards of the Bank for Export, the Agency for Industrial Development, and Autostrada Wielkopolska. He has been a permanent guest of the president during his state visits abroad.

Andrzej Arendarski, the leader of the Liberal Democratic Congress and minister of Cooperation with Foreign Countries in the Suchocka government of 1994 has become president of the Economic Chamber of Poland and a board member of Agros Holding, as well as vice president of Gas Trading Company and of Konsalnet, a firm founded by the former minister of interior, Jerzy Konieczny.

Prominent among the personalities who control and run the Polish economy is Jan Kulczyk, president of a major holding company in the agro-food business, motor industries, and telecommunications. Kulczyk is involved in all important state contracts, such as delivery of motor cars for state institutions, highway construction, and cellular telephones. He is head of the Polish Council of Businessmen, president of the brewery Lech Browary Wielopolskie and of Autostrada Wielkopolska, and a board member of the Warta Company. He was one of the two businessmen invited to the state dinner honoring Queen Elizabeth of Britain in Warsaw.

L'éminence grise of the new Polish establishment is Sobieslaw Zasada, a friend of all men in power. As such, he has succeeded in acquiring major government contracts (for example, Mercedes motor cars for the Armed Forces) and has been appointed as manager of a major arms industry with 11,000 employees.

Alexander Guzowaty is one of the richest men in Poland. He owns Bartimex, which specializes in trade with the West (in 1995, import-export exchanges reached 12 billion zlotys) and the West-European Bank and controls 25% of the Gas Trading shares. In the press he has been called "the man with his finger on the gas button."

Gradually, the banking business has been taking a leading role in the Polish economy. A prominent banker in full swing is Boguslaw Kott, president of the Economic Initiative Bank (BIG), which controls Bel Leasing (99.46% of shares), Big Bank SA (98% of shares), Bank Gdansky SA (26.7% of shares), and others. In the past, Kott was a director in the Ministry of Finance in charge of foreign trade. Currently, he is president of the Banking Council and a counselor of Premier Cimosewicz.

Like Kott, Stanislas Pacuk, president of Kredyt Bank SA, has joined the Democratic Left Alliance, the former governing party in Poland. Kredyt has recently become a big holding company, and Pacuk is a member of the board of quite a few companies, such as Budimex and Heros Insurance Company, as well as Glob Bank. He is a regular companion of President Kwasniewski on his visits abroad.

Other influential bankers are Cezary Stypulkowski, president of Commercial Bank; Marian Kanton, president of Pekao SA; Igor Chalupec, of the Polish Stock Market; Henryk Chmielac, president of the Warta Insurance Company and of Polish Investment Bank; Piotr Bykowski, president of Invest Bank and of Bank Staropolski, who worked closely with former prime minister Waldemar Pawlak. The change of government did not affect Bykowski's career; he is now the head of the advisers helping the minister of economic cooperation with foreign countries.

In general, most of the Polish plutocrats are not members of political parties; they prefer to maintain good relations with those in power, whatever their party. Some of them made a bet with those in power, and it seems they did not make a bad deal. This holds true for all the post-communist societies.

Especially striking is the fact that even in war-ravaged Bosnia, Croatia, and Serbia the same social mechanism is trying to assert itself. The only difference is the political power that is stubbornly fighting to keep the respective nation under control. In Serbia, for example, key elements of the economy—fuel, agriculture, industrial export-import—which were controlled by President Milosevic's cronies during the war, remain so after. The general manager of Progres, Serbia's largest export enterprise and the leading importer of Russian gas, is Prime Minister Mirko Marjanovic. The speaker of Parliament, Dragan Tomic, is the head of Yugopetrol, Serbia's major fuel distributor. Because such companies represent an enormous source of wealth, these politicians oppose both the market economy and foreign investors.

In all post-communist societies, we have found occupying important positions the political clans emanating from the old power structure. Their weight in each individual country varies according to specific local resources and conditions: the energy and raw material industries, the state arms and aerospace manufacturing groups, banking and financial interests, as well as the intelligence and security apparatus and regional, political, and economic establishments.

THE SIX CORRIDORS OF TOP MILLIONAIRES IN ROMANIA

In a gem of French literature, *Le corridor de la tentation,* Voltaire describes an ingenuous method of checking the honesty of men, inducing them to pass through a corridor of temptations, full of treasures so exposed as to allow easy theft. I was inspired by this model, reaching the conclusion that in Romania's transition period there have been six corridors of temptations leading to great wealth:

1. Corridor of Directocracy
2. Corridor of CEPEX (the former Politbureau)

3. Corridor of Export-Import
4. Corridor of Diaspora
5. Corridor of Self-Made Men
6. Corridor of Banks

Let us examine them one at a time.

Corridor of Directocracy

The term "directocracy," which was coined by Andrei Cornea, presupposes possession in the same hands of a state enterprise and a private company. The state sector is thus being used as a source of supply, of raw materials, and of all kinds of facilities to a private independent sector, whereby tremendous profits are achieved. Directly or through family members or friends quite a few state managers or directors possess companies or shares in the private sector. At the same time, by the very fact that they represent state interests in the economy, they enjoy close relations with the local administration and with the central authorities, the ministry, and other agencies. Thus, the political symbiosis between the party and the state has been replaced by an *economic symbiosis between the state and the private sector*. The transition has been carried out rapidly and without difficulties or resistance simply because the men representing the state then and now are the same.

In 1991, Traian Ciubotaru, general director, and Ion Iordan, chief bookkeeper of the firm S.C. Metalochimica in Iassy, transferred on credit commodities worth tens of million lei (read today, billions) to the companies created overnight: Util Casnic SRL and Fersatex SRL, the former belonging to Elena Ciubotaru, the director general's wife, and the latter to Silvia Iordan, the chief bookkeeper's wife, without getting any compensation. In the next three years, the two private firms flourished, whereas Metalochimica went bankrupt.

Nicolae Boambes, director of S.C. IMUC SA in Pitesti, which specializes in construction assembling, legally sold building materials and yielded contracts worth 175 million lei to the private company ICMA SRL whose owner was his wife Iuliana Boambes.

Mihai Porumbel, director of S.C. Agrotransport Oltenita, used 34 million lei from the company's assets to set up his private firm, Mobil SRL, also in Oltenita, specializing in import-export operations. In 1992, he took $6,187 in cash from the state company to make a trip to Czechoslovakia, where he purchased auto tires, signing the contract not for Agrotransport but for Mobil. In addition, he transferred to his own company $102 million from the state enterprise he managed.

Corridor of CEPEX

Members of the CEPEX (Political Executive Committee of Ceausescu) did not get directly involved in business because this was not tolerated. Instead, they usually resorted to relatives, nepotism flourishing in this era. Even bank deposits were made under the names of wives, sons, daughters, nephews, or sons-in-law on whose discretion they could rely. Therefore, as the prosecutors investigated bank accounts of CEPEX members, they found nothing in their names, and noted: "without wealth."

This model was set by the Ceausescus themselves. No bank deposits were found in their names, state coffers being at their disposal. However, as police inspectors searched the apartments of their sons Valentin and Nicu and daughter Zoia in early 1990, they found at each bank accounts worth 2 to 3 million lei, a real fortune at that time. Examining more carefully the dates of deposits, they noted that their careful mother, Elena, used to deposit 500,000 lei on each anniversary of their birthdays. Keep in mind that the average monthly wage was 2,000 lei.

Ion Dinca was one of the closest associates of Ceausescu. He married both his daughters to information engineers, despite Elena Ceausescu's hatred of the information revolution. When Professor Mihail Draganescu was sacked as director of the Romanian Institute of Information, one of Dinca's sons-in-law replaced him. This one was so grateful to his father-in-law that he took his name, Badea Dinca. All imports of electronics were made through this institute, so that Badea Dinca established good relations with the giants of electronics. After 1989, he knew how to turn these relations to good account, and this is how the powerful company Computerland was born. The other son-in-law, Gabriel Popoviciu, also turned to electronics; but, to avoid competition in the family, Computerland specialized in computers and software, while Popoviciu's Alltrom focused on precision balances and other electronic equipment. Eventually, the sons-in-law shook hands and signed a contract with the world chain of restaurants Pizza Hut; later, they bought the Dorobanti Hotel in Bucharest. Old Ion Dinca's lifetime struggle was not in vain: although he could not bring happiness to all Romanians, at least he did to his family.

Ion Ceausescu, the brother of the deceased Nicolae, and, as such, first vice president of the State Planning Committee, also had a daughter and, of course, a son-in-law, Marius Tarlea. Comrades knew how to select cadres, so that immediately after 1989, Marius Tarlea set up the company Eurotrading and started exporting urea on a large scale, making a fortune. With the dollars he earned, he founded in Zurich, Switzerland, the firm Manel Finanz AG, with assets worth 9 million Swiss francs, and started building in Bucharest the Columna Bank, which he launched on the market as a Romanian-Swiss bank.

In Nicu Ceausescu's orbit, as secretary of the Communist Youth, revolved two satellites more or less artificial: BTT (Bureau for Youth Tourism), with an enormous network of hotels, sport stadiums, and autocars (assets in 1994, 29.1 million lei), and UASCR (Union of Communist Student Associations), which proved after 1989 to be real pools of businessmen. Here is where Vasile Bostan got started, and he eventually became president of Columna Bank. This also launched Aurel Borsan, the director of BTT before and after 1989, who turned out to be the most diversified disciple of Nicu's—the founder of seven private companies: Dragon Medical Complex (1991), Business Affairs (1992), Rombulg (1992), Citadela (1992), Dacia Felix Tour (1992), Casino Est (1993), and Victoria International Enterprise Holding Corporation (1993).

Borsan did not forget his comrades: he attracted to Dacia Felix Tour, as shareholders, fifty-seven of them—all local department directors of BTT. Following the American saying "You scratch my back and I'll scratch yours," he got from Bancorex a 1,500,000-lei credit, guaranteed with BTT assets, which he transferred to Poolgec SRL, the business owned by George Paunescu, for an import of sugar and coffee whose profit they shared comradely. Although BTT is a tourist business, Borsan is not afraid of competition: Dacia Felix Tour, in which he invested 2,850,000 lei also specializes in the "organization of all kind of activities in national and international tourism." To demonstrate his generosity, Borsan added to this objective of Dacia: "purchasing of BTT shares." This is how the assets of this enormous holding company earned profits of many billion lei. Let us recognize that the "party's shift for tomorrow," as Ceausescu used to call the Communist Youth Union, has well deserved its historic mission.

Corridor of Export-Import

In the first five years after the revolution, the foreign trade sector handled operations worth over $80 billion. In 1995 alone, the trade exchanges of Romania exceeded $17 billion. In terms of personnel, this sector, in 1990, was the best equipped and qualified for the market economy. The staff had traveled in the West and in the Third World; they got to know industrialists, bankers, and businessmen; they spoke foreign languages fluently and knew the ropes of the game on world markets. Therefore, small wonder that after 1989 they fired the most spectacular "cannons" in the history of Romania's wild capitalism.

In the 1980s, forty-six foreign trade enterprises had functioned in Romania. They were run by a staff hired by a director general, specializing in various branches and activities, holding the monopoly in the respective branch. Their main source of revenue was the commission they got from each transaction, acting as intermediary between the Romanian state enterprises and foreign companies. Some of them, such as Industrial-importexport or Uzinexportimport, specialized in the construction of industrial plants abroad, particularly in the Middle East and Asia.

None of these forty-six enterprises possessed important buildings, fixed assets, or social capital, so after 1989 most of them were easily privatized through the MEBO method, people in executive positions remaining in the same chair. Actually, their most precious assets were the relations established with foreign companies and with Romanian enterprises specializing in producing export items and, of course, the kinds of skills acquired in foreign trade. Those who knew how to fructify this particular asset hit the jackpot and became millionaires in five years.

How did they do it? Through an ingenious model involving four moves. The first: privatization; the second: contacting the directors of factories and persuading them to continue producing the items in demand on world markets and exporting them through their good offices; the third: contacting foreign companies to continue doing business as usual; the fourth: reestablishing relations with banks, Romanian or foreign, that financed operations in the past. Of course, each of these moves succeeded by using "incentives" to persuade decision makers. In many cases, directors of foreign trade enterprises bought shares of producing factories, thus acquiring control over their business, or became board members of banks.

Romeo Pomponiu, director general of CONFEX, which specializes in ready-made clothes, has been an efficient businessman. He privatized his enterprise early in 1990, started making contacts with factories in Satu-Mare, Craiova, Sibiu, and Focsani, which he gradually bought one after another, and signed a contract with the giant German company Steilmann, which bought all his goods, while supplying the necessary textiles for manufacturing the clothes. In December 1989, the director general of Romano-Export was Petre Crişan. In 1990, he immediately privatized his enterprise, acquiring the lion's share: 55.9% of the social capital. Then he got control of two client firms, Duras-Nehoiu and Tricomontana, both specializing in woolen products. Gradually, Crişan bought controlling shares of fourteen factories, so that in 1994 Romano-Export reached a turnover of $14 million. With such a performance, Crişan qualified as minister of commerce in the Vacaroiu government, being authorized—among other things—to approve export and import licenses—the right man in the right place, as the English say.

At Tehnoforest in the 1980s a young man to watch was Viorel Cataramă. The enterprise used to export Romanian furniture to Western Europe, but young Cataramă displayed a special weakness for Belgium and the Netherlands, where he established close ties with the company ME Diffusion. He became its representative, and in 1984 he was promoted to director for Eastern Europe by the Belgian firm Belco. After the 1989 turnabout, Cataramă immediately decided to take advantage of the situation; he founded the company Elvila SRL and bought the plant Elmoberon, which exported 95% of its furniture production. Then he got control of the mattress factory Relaxa and built, in Bacau, the spinning mill Elbombix. This effort was not in vain, for in 1994 Elvila International was on top of the list of successful businesses with a $20 million turnover. For a while, Cataramă joined the government as undersecretary of commerce, but he claims that he considers himself chiefly as a businessman.

Foreign trade also attracted General Victor Atanasie Stanculescu. In 1959, as chief of supply section in the Ministry
of Defense for Supply and Procurement, Stanculescu handled intensively the business of import and export of arma-
ments and munitions. With the relations thus obtained in
Western business circles, after 1989 he became the representative of the British company Bali, founding, in Bucharest, the firm Bali Trading Company, which deals with
export-import affairs. Already in 1991 he had reached
a turnover of $20 to $22 million; and, in 1992, over $155
million. In association with Kay International, London, a
broker of Lloyds, Stanculescu set up the Anglo-Romanian
insurance company specializing in shipping, airlines, and
related fields.

Also from the foreign trade sector, George Constantin
Paunescu took off with the speed of a rocket. He started his
apprenticeship in the 1980s, in Milan, Italy, as chief of the
Commercial Agency of Romania, and then completed his education as director in the Ministry of Foreign Trade. With the
dollars accumulated "abroad" and relations in the Western
business circles, Paunescu, in 1991, set up the company Ages
SRL, with 152 items of export-import, and the firm Poolgec,
which organized exports of cement, steel-concrete, sugar,
rice, oil, cereals, and just about everything that was in demand on the domestic or foreign market. He pushed his
company to number four on the list of top enterprises in Romania. George Paunescu and his brother, Viorel, owner of
the nightclub Melody Bar, succeeded in buying the two
largest hotels in Bucharest, the Intercontinental and the
Lido, as well as the plush four-star hotel Rex in the Black Sea
resort of Mamaia. George Paunescu is the president of the
Union of Industrialists of Romania and is believed to be the
richest man in the country. A spectacular business hit was
the creation of a new airline, DACAIR, and the purchase of
twenty-four Canadian DASH-8 airplanes on a $425-million
credit loan from North American banks.

Dan Voiculescu also made a meteoric appearance in the Romanian business world. He started his career at Tehnoforest and then at Vitrocim, both export-import enterprises. Having established a solid financial basis in Cyprus with the company Crescent, he organized massive exports of cement and built Grifco International, a fine mechanical factory, which, in 1994, achieved the top position of industrial plants with a $5 million profit. Voiculescu imported modern printing equipment and became a sort of media mogul, with a daily newspaper, *Jurnalul National*, and a private TV company, Antena I. He acquired two personal jets and is considered to be in control of the most solid business holdings because, unlike his competitors, Voiculescu did not resort to huge bank credits, but made use of his own capital. In 1995 he created the Association of Businessmen, a handy instrument for establishing cozy relations with the government, and became its chairman.

Corridor of Diaspora

Quite a few Romanians who had emigrated to the West and made a fortune there came back after 1989 and started highly profitable businesses. The all-pervasive figure of Ion Tiriac dominates this scene. A former tennis player and manager of such champions as Boris Becker, Tiriac chose Germany as his favorite territory. Owing to vast relations in the business circles and to an exceptional intuition in investments (praised in the German press), Tiriac became a prosperous businessman with companies and houses in Frankfurt, New York, and Los Angeles and an annual profit estimated in 1993 at $100 million. Early in 1990, he returned to Romania and gradually set up the basis of a real empire. In cooperation with BERD, Tiriac founded the first private bank in Romania and a huge insurance company. He acquired the representation of Mercedes, Siemens, and Lufthansa; invested in numerous commercial and industrial enterprises;

and became involved in media affairs: a news agency, Mediafax, and a TV channel, PRO-TV, among others.

Another personality, famous as well as controversial, is Sever Muresan. A former tennis player at Dinamo and an officer in the security forces, he settled in France where he married a French woman with the approval of Romanian authorities, visiting Romania by car every year. After 1989, in a joint venture with the company Croissant de France, Muresan launched a chain of bakery stores, Panis. With a 16-million French franc credit from the Romanian Bank of Foreign Trade, he became a major shareholder and board member of the largest Romanian private bank, Dacia Felix. The company Invest Group, founded in Cluj, had assets worth $30 million in 1995, but as was revealed when Dacia Felix experienced a crisis that same year, Muresan had milked the bank of as much as a hundred billion lei.

Marcel Avram, who had left Romania for Israel in 1948 and eventually settled in Germany, became the owner of Mama Concerts, one of the world's largest impresario houses. After 1989, he set up the company Romasat, making his debut as a media mogul: the TV channel Tele7ABC, the radio station 2M+, and a partnership in the press trust Express.

In this same diaspora category should be listed such additional outstanding businessmen as Mihail Cărciog, the owner of the press trust Express and a major shareholder of Athénée Palace hotel and other enterprises; George Pădure, who returned from Belgium to found the major electric company GEPA; Alexander Feig, from Germany, the owner of the electronic firm Bucuresti-Berlin; Heinrich Schorsch, also from Germany, a major exporter of pigs and the owner of many factories producing salami and sausages in Timisoara, Baia Mare, and elsewhere; and a well-known industrialist from Italy, Iosif Constantin Drăgan, the owner of many newspapers and magazines and a shareholder in oil and gas companies.

Corridor of Self-Made Men

In the history of American electronics a romantic story stands out, that of engineer Steven Jobs who started the giant PC (personal computer) company Apple in a garage in Silicon Valley, California. Similarly in Romania, we have the case of a millionaire who started a workshop in a deserted stable of a cooperative farm. Constantin Toma studied the construction of machine tools in Galati and was promoted to foreman and chief-of-section in a metallurgical plant. After 1989, with only 100,000 lei in his pocket and with eight fellow workers, he started a small factory in a stable to produce Aquator water purifiers, which were based on their own inventions. They sold the purifiers very well, both in domestic and foreign markets. Swiftly, Toma built a new factory, Emaflux, to produce halogen lamps, followed by six other factories manufacturing wrought iron, inox, and thermal products. These were eventually merged into a huge holding, ROMET, which made him the richest man in the Buzau department. Taking advantage of the new law that made each invention patent-tax exempt, Toma did spend 500 million lei for research and, as he admitted, only in 1994 did he enjoy a one-billion lei profit.

At the top of this list of magnates rising from below are without any doubt, George Copos and his wife–co-entrepreneur, Ana. As a member of the International Federation of Youth, Copos had enjoyed the opportunity to travel in Western countries and to observe *sur le vif* how business was working in a market economy. In 1990, he created the famous bakery and pastry shop Ana, which very rapidly expanded into a chain in Bucharest. Concluding a happy joint venture with the South Korean giant Samsung, Copos established the company Ana Electronic and imported machinery to produce computers and other electronic items in Bucharest. His profit in 1995 was estimated at $40 million.

Gelu Tofan worked for five years at the tire factory Danubiana. After 1989, along with a partner and a modest capital of $50,000 sent by his brother from Canada, he bought a big truck and started selling tires all over the country. After only one year, he opened twelve stores to sell tires in major cities. His turnover rose rapidly: 30 million lei in 1992, 6 billion in 1993, 48 billion in 1994, and over 100 billion in 1995.

Cristian Tăntăreanu was born in the village of Corbeanca, which he decided to put on the world map. A construction engineer, he was employed in the 1980s as director at the Trust for Special Works and Technological Insulation. After 1989, he started building a large shopping center, Prisma, on the Bucharest-Ploiesti highway, with six hundred small shops that sold all kinds of merchandise at attractive prices. In association with McDonald's, Amico, and others, he set up a construction company to build residential suburban-type houses in various parts of the country.

Corridor of Banks

In the world today, financial capital reigns over the market and therefore exercises an extraordinary attraction to all those who dream of getting rich. Not even the best industrialist or merchant can make a $1-billion profit in one day, as magnate Soros did by a formidable stock exchange hit. Not surprisingly, in Romania, too, after 1989, banks, mutual funds, and investment companies, not to mention pyramidal crooks, appeared like mushrooms after the rain.

In launching an industrial or commercial enterprise one can make use of one's position as director, fructify business relations, or get bank credits, but the creation of a bank requires a large amount of money from the very beginning. Where could one obtain that in Ceausescu's Romania? This is the puzzle we have to clarify. What kind of people were those who founded private banks in Romania?

From the viewpoint of capital, there are in Romania today three types of banks: state, private, and cooperatist. Their assets, credits, deposits, and profits (in billion lei), as of December 31, 1994, are illustrated in Table 5.

The founders and managers of private banks, with the exception of Ion Tiriac, have been coming from the financial *state apparatus* of the communist regime. Marcel Ivan, president of Credit Bank, was the director of the Ilfov subsidiary of Banca Agricola; Ion Sima, president of Bank Dacia Felix, worked at the Investment Bank of Cluj; Banca Românească is headed by Gheorghe Crăiniceanu, the former president of BRCE, and by Dumitru Lăzăroiu, a former director in the Ministry of Finance; Dinulescu, the manager of Bankcoop, was president of the Credit House of Consumer Cooperative, and Prundus and Radu, managers of Mindbank, were board members of BRCE.

None of those possessed the necessary billions to set up a bank, so again the source of private banks was the *state capital* of the state enterprises involved. Marcel Ivan built Credit Bank with the massive subscription of capital by Intercontinental Hotel, Romcereal, and other state enterprises, while Dacia Felix was brought to life with the capital of Electroaparataj, Nord Conforest, ASTRA, ARCOM, F.P.P. Transilvania, and others. An examination of the list of shareholders of private banks will reveal the names of major state enterprises. Of course, after the initial capitalization, many citizens bought shares or deposited money. In the case of the two cooperatist banks, the problem was simpler, as the capital of former cooperatives already existed.

Most of the banks rapidly became active on the financial market, and, as can be seen in Table 5, in 1994 they made substantial profits: for example, 138 billion lei, Banca Comerciala Romana; 98 billion lei, BRD; and 82 billion lei, Bancorex. There have also been scandalous irregularities in their operations, such as big credits of tens and hundreds of billion lei granted without proper guarantees, or the irresponsible ma-

Table 5
Status of Romanian Banks, December 31, 1994 (in billion lei)

	Total Assets	Credits Granted	Deposits	Net Profit
State				
Banca Comerciala Romana	2,998,208	2,011,654	2,084,532	138,525
Bancorex (BRCE)	3,227,687	2,060,500	1,624,857	82,880
Banca Agricola	4,471,136	3,483,022	1,118,581	32,795
Banca Romana pentru Dezvoltare (BRD)	1,383,168	586,426	992,669	98,408
Casa de Economii si Consemnatiuni	1,603,600	953,800	1,049,000	51,800
Banc Post	408,126	72,709	309,993	19,825
Cooperatist				
Bankcoop	587,488	335,942	140,484	6,665
Mindbank	74,667	11,725	35,192	7,348
Private				
Banca Ion Tiriac	454,504	232,332	345,158	15,475
Banca Dacia Felix	1,528,496	488,590	580,489	18,354
Banca Romaneasca	18,977	3,073	6,535	1,006
Banca Internationala a Religiilor	85,864	11,719	24,927	2,745
Credit Bank	[in trouble, threatening bankruptcy]			
Columna Bank	[created in 1995]			

nipulation of people's deposits in the activities of Dacia Felix and Credit Bank. These activities required the drastic intervention of the National Bank, which is legally authorized to control the operations of all banks—state or private.

One such report of the National Bank showed that Dacia Felix in 1994 recorded losses of more than 60 billion lei and yet reported a profit of 21.1 billion lei, thus paying dividends of 11.1 billion. The same report revealed that 97% of credits were granted without observing the legal conditions, so that in 1995 the losses of Dacia Felix exceeded 530 billion lei.

THE SYMBIOSIS OF POWER AND CAPITAL

How do changes in the social configuration of the nation affect the political spectrum? As we have seen, 1990 and 1991 were years of petrification of the old social structure in Romania and only at the end of 1992, as a result of sudden changes in economic life, did a first dislocation of that structure occur. In the May 1990 elections, the workers and peasants dominated the popular vote, so that "a president for our serenity" received 85% of the popular vote. In the local elections of 1992 modifications in Romanian society were already being felt. Liberalization of prices and foreign trade; privatization of commerce, small industry and services; and the agrarian reform—all shook up the old social relations and inaugurated a process of deep social transformation. The working class declined numerically and lost its social position and prestige, being hit by rising prices and the specter of unemployment. This explains why candidates of the opposition won the mayorships in big urban centers, particularly in Bucharest.

Sociologist Petre Datculescu noted: "The rural population and that of small towns had common interests. These social groups were positively affected by the land reform initiated under Iliescu's presidency. . . . But faced with enormous difficulties and uncertainties about losing their land, the new owners wanted the strong support of the state. Electing Ion Iliescu, they hoped that the state would alleviate some of their difficulties, helping them to be prosperous and save their property."[9] In other words, on the social plane also, Romania was in a transition period, though this was a transition less rapid and somewhat belated as compared with that in the political and economic spheres. This gap was reflected in the political spectrum. The lack of social crystallization impaired the natural endeavor of each political party to identify its social basis, to represent and defend its interests, and to cultivate it in order to get its electoral support. Under such conditions, notions such as left, center, and right, which make sense in a definite social structure, suffer from ambiguity, thus explaining the reluctance of political parties to assert categorically that they are on the left or the right of the political spectrum—all choosing instead to stick to the center. Even leftist parties have avoided taking radical stances.

The Democrat Party, a splinter of FSN, became social-democratic, although in 1991 the Roman government had adopted a reformist neo-liberal program. PNT renounced the peasant orientation, espousing Christian democracy. Finally, PRM and PUNR, inheritors of Ceausescu's national communism, adopted nationalist-chauvinistic positions, resorting to the rightist ideological verbiage. The electoral campaign of 1996 for the first time reflected the appearance of the new social forces in embryo: the *middle class*, and its superior stratum, the *capitalists*. These social forces are now coloring part of the political spectrum, determining more articulate assertions in the programs of political parties and causing significant oscillations in the power structure. The big capitalists own newspapers and magazines, radio stations and TV channels thus becoming a major factor in influencing public opinion and the electorate.

The liberal party PL'93 proclaimed the principle *restitutio in integrum*, that all nationalized properties should be given back to their owners. Its leader, Dinu Patriciu, declared, in

Lady Margaret Thatcher style, that he would not accept paying $55 for a ton of coal extracted in Valea Jiului at a time when its price on the world market was $25. Emil Constantinescu, who in 1992 asked for the "vote of the poor," now asserts that the Democratic Convention is the rightist alternative to the Vacaroiu government and has developed a "Contract with Romania" program inspired by the conservative republicans in the United States.

But the most striking mutation is to be found in the evolution of power. Prime Minister Vacaroiu defended to the last ditch his minister of commerce, Petre Crişan, despite the fact that the latter was unmasked in the press for being the owner or manager of sixteen entreprises. President Iliescu started participating in the inauguration of new luxury hotels and in festivities of some joint ventures, something he did not do in 1990 and 1992.

Actually, I found it quite natural that the mutation should take place in the sector most directly affected by the emergence of new social forces at the peak of society's pyramid— power. The major industrialists, merchants, or bankers could not possibly make a fortune and assert themselves on the social plane without the support of those in power. In turn, those who hold power cannot isolate themselves from the new social milieu that is taking shape around them, and they can hardly resist the temptation to get involved more or less directly in the business profits being made under their noses and, in fact, at their hands. *The symbiosis between power and capital is a main feature of the transition period.* The fact, so amply demonstrated in this book, that the formation of the new capitalist class has been achieved mainly at the expense of the state, the owner of the most important resources of the country, leads to the conclusion that the power-capital symbiosis, far from being accidental, is the result of a *social process both necessary and inevitable.* The representatives of the executive and legislative power will, of course, find the ways and means to arrange for that "holy alliance" conditions of perfect legality in the state of law.

The extraordinary strength shown by this symbiosis in defending its right to exist was manifest in February and March 1995, as the parliament rejected Article 7 of the proposed Law of the Status of Deputies and Senators, which provided for the interdiction of legislators to participate on boards or at shareholders' meetings of state enterprises. What does a board member mean in terms of money?

The contract for such members provides:

1. 25,000 lei plus travel expenses for each meeting
2. 50,000 lei for each million that exceeds the dividend
3. 50,000 lei for each million that recuperates the loss sustained in the initial stage
4. 50,000 lei for the maintenance of the dividend level.

As members of the boards have cashed in tens of millions, some even hundreds of millions, it was decided that the payment "will not exceed 2.5 times the salary of the manager or director general." Keeping in mind that such salaries reach 2–3 million lei monthly, the limit for a board member is 5–7 million lei monthly. To mention but one case, at Oil Terminal Constanta, as a result of a 5-billion lei profit in 1994, each board member received 150 million lei for that year.

But deputies and senators are members of many boards and shareholders' meetings. Ioan Dumitrescu (PDSR), a member of the House and vice president of the Anti-Corruption Commission, when accused of being a member of six boards, retorted with indignation: "I am not in 6, but only in 4 boards, and my wife only in 3."[10] His four were SC Mamaia, Naval Shipyard 2 May-Mangalia, SC Vinvico, and SC Olympus; his wife's: SC Agiloc, Avicola SA, Agigea, and Sorena SA. With regard to their involvement in those enterprises, the same deputy, Dumitrescu, declared: "I got for Navrom a credit of $11 million; together with minister Mihailescu we took the ships of Ilempa, which had $1 million debt to Navrom and gave them to the firm Ritz-Rom which paid the debt: I helped naval shipyard

2 May-Mangalia to make contact with the South Korean company Daewoo; I helped SC Vinvico to enter the Swedish market, and at SC Mamaia I contributed the conclusion of some tourist arrangements with foreign travel agencies." One could hardly tell the difference between a deputy and a businessman!

The following is a list of legislators who are board members in the following departments:

Alba:	Maier Ion, deputy, PDSR—Cetatea SA and PECO Alba
Arges:	Rizescu Gheorghe, senator, PDSR—Cara SA
	Simionescu Constantin, Senator, PDSR—Arpechim SA
	Jugrafu Marin, deputy, PDSR—Conmus SA
	Nistor Iulian, deputy, PDSR—ARO SA, ARPO SA
Botosani:	Mocanu Dumitru, senator, PDSR—Luceafarul
	Moldovan Constantin, senator, PRM—Condacia
Braila:	Broscateanu Ion, senator, PDSR—PECO SA
	Matetovici Mihai, senator, PDSR—Promex SA
	Petre Petrica, deputy, PDSR—Blubedex SA, Vinalcool SA
Constanta:	Anton Marin Mangiurea, deputy, PDSR—Eforie SA
	Mihai Lita, deputy, PDSR—Carmego SA, Fluriveg SA
	Gheorghe Dumitrascu, senator, PDSR—Libramaris SA
Dolj:	Andrei Potcoava, senator, PL'93—Craimodex SA, Elpreco SA
Mehedinti:	Nicolae Serdin, deputy, PDSR—PECO SA, Merva SA, Drobeta SA
	Eugen Nicolcea, deputy, PDSR—Medro SA, Severnav SA

In March 1995, when the issue was discussed in the House and Ion Predescu, chairman of the Juridical Commission, argued in favor of Article 7, only a few deputies supported the amendment and the project was buried.

As in Poland, both President Iliescu and Prime Minister Vacaroiu have been accompanied during their visits abroad by such businessmen as George Paunescu, Viorel Catarama, Dan Voiculescu, General Stanculescu, and George Copos. Actually, the power-capital symbiosis functions more or less transparently and now runs the state in all post-communist societies. Capital was grabbed from the state.

In Russia, president Yeltsin has let business clans rip off the nation's gas, oil, minerals, and noble metals. Viktor Cernomyrdin, the prime minister he anointed, is the godfather of Gazprom, the giant gas monopoly whose turnover is bigger than that of General Motors. The cozy relationship between the Kremlin and big business was illustrated by the elevation of Alexei Nikolaev, president of the Volga automobile factory to the post of first deputy prime minister; as previously mentioned, after General Lebed's drastic ouster, one of Russia's richest businessmen and a major backer of Yeltsin's re-election campaign, Boris Berezovski, was appointed deputy chief of the National Security Council. It is not surprising that Lebed, at a press conference, shot at Chernomyrdin: "Raw materials capital has become so independent from the state that it has begun to conduct its own budget, credit, monetary and regional policy." The general does not understand that big business is not independent of the state: it *is* the state.

Big businessmen come in and out of the Kremlin: Vladimir Potanin, Alexei Nikolaev, and Boris Berezevski (worth $3 billion according to *Fortune*) have all held important positions in the government. Victor Cernomyrdin remains as prime minister.

The power-capital symbiosis is at work even in war-ravaged Yugoslavia. The economic sanctions imposed by the United Nations on Yugoslavia during the war fostered huge black-market schemes run by top aides of President Slobodan Milosevic to smuggle goods such as gasoline into the country. Although the sanctions were lifted when the war ended in 1995, those who took control of the state-run industries have not released their grip on their financial empires.

Zoran Todorovic, age 38, also known as "Rifle Butt" for his savage methods of persuasion, was a close associate of the president and his wife, Mirijana Markovic, often dining at their home. He was among the communist officials who helped Milosevic rise to power a decade ago. For his services he obtained a monopoly over all oil imports into Yugoslavia. He had vast real estate holdings and was reputed to be one of the richest men in Yugoslavia.

Another top Milosevic associate was Vlada Kovacevic, known as "Spade." He ran a string of duty-free shops, owned some ten companies and, like many close to the president, was able to import goods without having to pay the stiff tariffs imposed on those without connections to the top. It was no surprise that Kovacevic was killed in front of Belgrade's largest shopping mall, apparently as part of the struggle within the ruling elite for control of the state-run industries and vast black-market rings.

Epilogue: Whither Russia and Eastern Europe?

A recent public opinion poll regarding the future of Romania revealed that 50% of its citizens did not know where the country was heading, while 40% were divided as follows: 15%—toward *capitalism*, 11%—toward *western socialism*; 13%—toward *restoration of communism*. Why such confusion?

After the 1989 revolution in Eastern Europe, political leaders chose to talk about the way toward democracy and a market economy without indicating that these two historical tasks could not be implemented in their contemporary world but only within a capitalist social system. After so many decades of demonizing the defects of capitalism, leaders did not dare to mention it. However, gradually Romanian society, as well as Polish and Hungarian societies, have acquired the features characteristic of capitalism, although in the economy state ownership maintains an important place. On the social plane, the polarization of society has become increasingly apparent: at one pole, millions of people beset by poverty, unemployment, and misery; at the other pole, the billionaires and millionaires with their fabulous profits, living in luxury and glamour. In between, the middle class is taking shape: the stabilizing factor in modern society.

This social evolution has been strongly stimulated by the international environment in which Romania and other Eastern European nations entered after the collapse of the communist bloc. In fact, the *integration into the Euro-Atlantic structures* is the supreme strategic objective of all these countries as well as the basic condition of their political and economic development. Whoever is in power—center right or center left—will follow the same strategic objective. The fact that in Poland and Hungary center-left governments made up chiefly of ex-communists have carried on with equal determination the march towards capitalism proves once again that the Euro-Atlantic objective and the political urge to fulfill its requisites constitute the decisive factor in the evolution of those societies.

Not so in the case of Russia. Apparently, Russia's way will depart from that of Eastern European nations. Indeed, *while the mechanism of the world economic system compels Eastern European nations to play by the rules of the world market, the referee being the International Monetary Fund, the dynamics of power politics generates in a great power like Russia the will to resist, and gradually oppose, the tendency of the Western Powers to assert their supremacy.*

The workings of the modern world system is such that it creates in each historical period anti-systemic forces within its scope. The 1917 October Revolution, rather than being a socialist revolution, was the anti-systemic reaction of a backward peasant nation against the industrial system of the West, and Stalin's slogan "socialism in one country" was a desperate attempt to disconnect Russia from that overpowering world system in order to industrialize it. So, today, there is an anti-systemic reaction in Russia's resistance against the pressure coming from the West to make it accept the latter's model of society, thus co-opting Russia into the system.

The assumption that the market economy combined with democratic pluralism and freedoms will tame the traditional Russian expansionism and national eagerness, allowing the

West to steer the further course of Russia, has proved to be wrong and deceptive. The new parliament, precisely because it reflects the nation's choice, is poised not only against the restoration of capitalism, but also against the Western model of democracy. The Duma's decision of February 1994 to grant amnesty to the communist putchists was a major setback for the fragile Russian democracy and state of law.

Seven decades of systematic suppression of freedom and initiative, of ideological indoctrination demonizing free enterprise, have left a mind-set that will take at least a generation to alter. Never throughout their history have Russians experienced a period of democracy. Already in 1904, historian P. Miliukov had noted: "In Russia, the State exerted enormous influence upon the social organization, whereas in the West, the social organization conditioned the state system." The weakening of state control in recent years, instead of giving rise to a civil society, has fostered crime, drug addiction, and lawlessness on an alarming scale. There is a wide popular demand for the restoration of law and order. Above all, the national pride has suffered a terrible trauma: the sudden downfall from the status of a superpower, equal only to the United States of America, to Yeltsin's Russia, which looks like a poor relative accepted at the dinner table of the Seven Rich, on an additional chair. Therefore, when Zhirinovsky and Rutskoi speak of a "Greater Russia" and accuse Gorbachev and Yeltsin of having sold out to the West, they strike a sensitive chord. That special message could not be ignored by Yeltsin. He now claims that Russia "remains a superpower" and rejects being treated as a junior partner.

The mystique of "Holy Russia" runs deep in the nation's soul and mind. The Russians, cherishing communitarian values rather than the Western cult of individual liberty and lacking industriousness or pragmatism, are endowed instead with a unique spirituality and sense of mission, feeling that they are different and have a destiny of their own. Hence, the realization is growing in the country that the way of the West is not for Russia, that Russia must follow a course of its own. The political leaders who will chart such a course before the nation will enjoy popular support. And a strong presidential system, rather than a parliamentary type of government, is a historical necessity in Russia.

Moscow's attempts to reconstruct the Soviet Union have failed twice and they are going to fail in the future. The leaders of the new independent republics will never accept a political-military scheme that will return them to the status of a Russian *gubernia*. They have enjoyed the prerogatives of independence, particularly the role of actors on the international scene, and they are not going to renounce them. Moreover, the republics possessing major natural resources, such as oil-rich Azerbaijan or Kazakhstan, are anxious to exploit these sources of wealth for their own good, even at the risk of military confrontation, as the case of Chechnya has amply demonstrated. Belarus, the only republic that seemed at one moment to be moving toward union with the Russian Federation, has practically given up the idea.

Although some sort of economic union, particularly with the republics dependent on Russian oil and gas, should not be excluded, this is unlikely to bring either union with Russia or capitalism in Russia. To sum up: although the capitalist system will extend throughout the whole area of the former communist bloc, the Western model of democracy will stop short at the Russian border.

Notes

CHAPTER 1

1. Quoted in Murray Yanovich, *Social and Economic Inequality in the Soviet Union* (New York: Sharpe, 1977), p. 5.

2. O. I. Shkaratan, *Problemy sotsial'noi structury rabochego klassa SSR* (Moscow, 1970), p. 153.

3. Walter D. Connor, *Socialism, Politics and Equality* (New York: Columbia University Press, 1979), pp. 79–80.

4. Ibid., p. 80.

5. Milovan Djilas, *The New Class* (New York: Praeger, 1960).

6. Leonard Schapiro, *The Communist Party of the Soviet Union* (New York, 1960).

7. Jan Szczepanski, *Polish Society* (New York: Random House, 1970).

8. Walter D. Connor, p. 104.

CHAPTER 2

1. *Rabochii Klass i sovremennie mir*, Moscow, No. 6, 1986.

2. W. Weselowski, "The Notions of Class and Strata in Socialist Societies," in *The Social Structure of Eastern Europe,* ed. Bernard Lewis (New York: Praeger, 1976), p. 6.

3. John Naisbit, *Megatrends* (New York: Warner Books, 1982), p. 14.

4. *Rabochii Klass.*

5. Ibid.

6. Ibid.

7. Radovan Richta, *Civilizatia la rascruce* (Bucharest: Ed. Politica, 1970), p. 47.

8. *La Recherche,* Paris, No. 14 (July–August 1981), p. 614.

9. Tatiana Zaslavskaya, "The Human Factor in the Development of Socialist Economy and Socialist Equity," *Kommunist,* September 1986, pp. 61–73.

10. Radovan Richta, p. 288.

11. *New Times,* Moscow, No. 12, 1986, p. 12.

12. Mikhail Gorbachev, *On the Tasks of the Party in Restructuring of Economic Management* (Moscow: Novosti, 1987).

13. Interview with L. A. Kostin, first vice president of the Committee of Labor, *Pravda,* February 17, 1987.

14. Mikhail Gorbachev, p. 54.

15. "Good-bye to Wage Leveling," *Moscow News,* No. 1, 1988.

16. Ibid.

17. Tatiana Zaslavskaya.

18. Interview L. A. Kostin.

19. Ibid.

20. Ivan T. Berend and Gyorgy Ranki, *The Hungarian Economy in the Twentieth Century* (New York: St. Martin's Press, 1985), p. 244.

21. Nikolay Schmeliov, "Only the Market Place," reprinted from *Novy Mir,* June 1987.

22. Mikhail Gorbachev, p. 54.

23. *New Times,* Moscow, November 1987, p. 12.

24. Mikhail Gorbachev, *Speech in Murmansk* (Moscow: Novosti, 1987), p. 17.

25. K. A. Shabeikov, *Pravovye formy oplaty truda v kholkozkh* (Moscow, 1963), p. 225.

26. Merwin Matthews, *Class and Society in Soviet Russia* (New York: Walker, 1982).

27. Zygmunt Bauman, "Social Dissent in the Eastern European System," in *The Social Structure of Eastern Europe*, ed. Bernard Lewis (New York: Praeger, 1976), p. 125.

28. Krzystof Zagorski, "Social Mobility in Poland," ibid., p. 80.

29. Ibid., p. 82.

30. Zygmunt Bauman, p. 54.

31. Quoted in David Lane, *Soviet Economy and Society* (New York: New York University Press, 1985), pp. 278–79.

32. Mikhail Gorbachev, *Speech to C.C. of CPSU*, January 1987 (Moscow: Novosti).

33. Interview with L. A. Kostin.

34. Tatiana Zaslavskaya.

35. Abraham Bergson and Herbert S. Levine, *The Soviet Economy toward the Year 2000* (London: Allen and Unwin, 1983), p. 337.

36. Radovan Richta, p. 289.

37. Ota Sik, "Czechoslovakia's New System of Economic Planning and Management," *Eastern European Economics*, Fall 1965, p. 22.

38. Vaclav Muller, "The Price of Egalitarianism," *Problems of Communism*, July–August 1969, p. 48.

39. W. Weselowski, p. 14.

40. Ibid., pp. 14–15.

41. Charles Bettelheim, "On the Transition between Capitalism and Socialism," *Monthly Review*, March 1969.

42. Frank Parkin, "Market Socialism and Class Structure," in *The Social Structure of Eastern Europe*, ed. Bernard Lewis (New York: Praeger, 1976), pp. 34–35.

43. Ibid., p. 38.

44. Ibid., p. 40.

45. Ibid., p. 43.

46. George Konrad and Ivan Szeleny, *The Intellectuals on the Road to Power* (New York: Harcourt Brace Jovanovich, 1979), preface, p. xv.

47. Ibid.

48. Anthony Giddens, *The Class Structure of Advanced Societies* (London: Hutchinson, 1973), p. 249.

49. Frank Parkin, "System Contradiction and Political Transformation," *European Journal of Sociology*, No. 13, 1972, p. 50.

50. David Lane, *The Socialist Industrial State* (London: Allen and Unwin, 1976), pp. 94–95.

51. *Perestroika, kto za, kto protiv?* Moscow: Nedelia, 1988.

52. *Beijing Review*, No. 45, 1987, pp. xvi, xx.

53. Leonard Shapiro, *The Communist Party of the Soviet Union* (New York: Random House, 1960), p. 343.

CHAPTER 3

1. Max Lerner, *America as a Civilization* (New York: Simon and Schuster, 1957), p. 488.

2. Ibid., p. 494.

3. Eric Hobsbawm, *Age of Extremes* (London: Michael Joseph, 1994).

4. C. Wright Mills, *White Collar* (Oxford: Oxford University Press, 1953), p. ix.

5. Rudolf Andorka, "Hungarian Society: Heritage of the Past, Problems of the Transition and Possible Future Development up to 2005," in *Society and Economy in Central and East Europe* (Budapest: Budapest University of Economic Sciences), 1995.

6. I. Szeleny, "Embourgeoisement in Hungary: National Propertied Bourgeoisie and Intelligentsia in the Process of Embourgeoisement," *Valosag*, Vol. 33, No. 1, pp. 30–41.

7. David Remnick, "Letter from Moscow: The Tycoon and the Kremlin," *New Yorker*, February 20–27, 1995, p. 130.

8. Ibid.

9. Irsop, Bucharest, 1992.

10. *Adevarul*, March 4–5, 1995.

Selected Bibliography

Andorka, Rudolf. "Hungarian Society: Heritage of the Past, Problems of Transition up to 2005," in *Society and Economy in Central and East Europe*. Budapest: Budapest University of Economic Sciences, 1995.

Berend, Ivan T., and George Ranki. *The Hungarian Economy in the Twentieth Century*. New York: St. Martin's Press, 1985.

Bergson, Abraham, and Herbert S. Levine. *The Soviet Economy toward the Year 2000*. London: Allen and Unwin, 1983.

Brucan, Silviu. *World Socialism at the Crossroads*. New York: Praeger Publishers, 1987.

Bullok, Allan. *Hitler and Stalin, Parallel Lives*. New York: Alfred A. Knopf, 1992.

Cohen, Stephen. *Bukharin and the Bolshevik Revolution*. New York: Alfred A. Knopf, 1973.

Connor, Walter. *Socialism, Politics and Equality*. New York: Columbia University Press, 1979.

Darwish, Karen, and Bruce Parrott, eds. *Democratization and Authoritarianism in Post-Communist Societies*. Cambridge: Cambridge University Press, 1997.

Djilas, Milovan. *The New Class*. New York: Praeger Publishers, 1960.

Fejtö, F. *Histoire des democraties populaires*. Paris: Le Seuil, 1972.

Filipov, F. R. *Sociologia obrazovaniia*. Moscow: Nauk, 1980.

Furet, Francois. *Le passé d'une illusion*. Paris: Robert Lafont/ Calman Levy, 1995.

Frydman, Roman, Kenneth Murphy, and Andrzej Rapaczynski, eds. *Capitalism with a Comrade's Face*. Central European University Press, distributed in the United States by Cornell Services.

Giddens, Anthony. *The Class Structure of Advanced Societies*. London: Hutchinson, 1973.

Hobsbawm, Eric. *Ages of Extremes*. London: Michael Joseph, 1994.

Keren, Michael, and Gur Ofer, eds. *Economic Reform in the Former Communist Bloc*. Boulder: CO: Westview Press, 1992.

Konrad, George, and Ivan Szeleny. *The Intellectuals on the Road to Power*. New York: Harcourt Brace Jovanovich, 1979.

Lane, David. *Soviet Economy and Society*. New York: New York University Press, 1985.

Lewis, Bernard, ed. *The Social Structure of Eastern Europe*. New York: Praeger Publishers, 1976.

Marx, Karl. *Capital*, 3 vols. Moscow: 1961.

Matthews, Merwin. *Class and Society in Soviet Russia*. New York: Walker, 1982.

Medvedev, Roy A. *Let History Judge*. New York: Alfred A. Knopf, 1972.

Mills, C. Wright. *White Collar*. New York: Oxford University Press, 1953.

Mungiu, Alina. *Romanii dupa '89*. Bucharest: Humanitas, 1995.

Richta, Radovan, ed. *Civilizatia la rascruce*. Bucharest: Politica, 1970.

Shakhnazarov, G. K. *Sotsialisticheskaya demokratsia: nekotorye voprosy theorii*, 2nd ed. Moscow: Polizdat, 1974.

Szczepanski, Jan. *Polish Society*. New York: Random House, 1970.

Szeleny, I. *Embourgeoisement in Hungary*, vol. 33, no. 1. Budapest: Valosag, 1995.

Yanovitch, Murray. *Social and Economic Inequality in the Soviet Union*. New York: Sharpe, 1977.

Zaslavski, Victor. *The Neo-Stalinist State*. New York: Sharpe, 1982.

Index

116

About the Author

SILVIU BRUCAN has had a long and distinguished career as an activist, diplomat, and scholar. He participated in the anti-fascist underground during World War II and was a leading dissident of the Ceausescu dictatorship and one of the leaders of the revolution of December 1989. He served as Romania's ambassador to the United States (1956–59) and to the United Nations (1959–62). He is the author of six earlier books in English, including *The Wasted Generation* and *Pluralism and Social Conflict* (Praeger, 1990).

ISBN 0-275-96322-5

90000>

EAN

9 780275 963224

HARDCOVER BAR CODE